GEORGE MACKAY BROWN is remembered for his poetry, novels, plays and short stories. Much of his fiction and verse was based on his life in Orkney, especially his childhood. He was born in Stromness, Orkney, in 1921. He was at Newbattle Abbey College when Edwin Muir was Warden. He read English at Edinburgh University and did postgraduate work on Gerard Manley Hopkins.

He was awarded an Arts Council grant for poetry in 1965, The Society of Authors' Travel Award in 1968, The Scottish Arts Council Literature Prize in 1969 for *A Time to Keep*, and the Katherine Mansfield Menton Short Story Prize in 1971. He was awarded the OBE in January 1974.

He received honorary degrees from the Open University (MA), Dundee University (LLD), Glasgow University (DLitt) and he was a fellow of the Royal Society of Literature. In 1987 his novel *The Golden Bird* won the James Tait Black prize. George Mackay Brown died in 1996.

Letters
from
Hamnavoe

George Mackay Brown

Steve Savage
London and Edinburgh

Steve Savage Publishers Ltd
The Old Truman Brewery
91 Brick Lane
LONDON
E1 6QL

www.savagepublishers.com

Published in Great Britain by Steve Savage Publishers Ltd 2002

First published in hardback by Gordon Wright Publishing Ltd 1975
Copyright © George Mackay Brown 1975

ISBN 1-904246-01-X

British Library Cataloguing in Publication Data
A catalogue entry for this book is available from the British Library

Cover photograph: Gordon Wright

Typeset by Steve Savage Publishers Ltd
Printed and bound by The Cromwell Press Ltd

Contents

Introduction

These short essays were written over a period of years for *The Orcadian* newspaper. They appeared every Thursday at the foot of a column of Stromness news (not written by me) which included obituaries, reports of whist drives, weddings, old folks' outings, etc. The intention of the 'Letter from Hamnavoe' was to entertain a small community of 1,600 townsfolk—possibly a scattering of other islanders—also to kindle home thoughts in the minds of the thousands of Orkney folk who live outwith the islands but keep in touch through the pages of the paper.

From time to time somebody or other would say 'I think there should be a book made of them', and I would reply rather vaguely; and then nothing more would be heard of it for another six months or so.

Brian Murray, Adviser in English to Ayrshire Education Committee, was not to be put off so lightly. When he and Gordon Wright the publisher came together in Orkney in the summer of 1974, the question of making a book of a selection of the 'Letters' was seriously aired. It was one lucent still evening in the lounge of the Braes Hotel, with its marvellous outlook over Orphir, Scapa Flow and Hoy, that the three of us went into the matter. They were more determined about it than I was. These 'Letters' (I protested) were never meant to be given the permanence of book covers; far less to be 'cuttings in stone' (which presumably is the aim of every serious poet); they were light reading for quiet townsfolk on a Thursday afternoon, and as ephemeral as the newsprint they gossiped, whimsied, and reminisced out of.

Still (I conceded) if a rigorous selection of the best of them were made, it might make a pleasant bedside book even for readers outside Orkney.

Here, then, is the result. Those who look to have 'real issues' discussed—like oil, fishing, tourism, agriculture—will find nothing to get their teeth into. There is little about politics or religion either —these attract hosts of 'Letters to the Editor', and I have neither the energy nor the desire to take part in such barren scuffles.

Readers will notice how vividly northerners are aware of the quartered year with its equinoxes and solstices. Immense tides of light and darkness are woven into our existence.

There is a great deal of reminiscence; not only shreds of nostalgia for my own childhood, 'the vision splendid', but for the simpler and more meaningful community that Orkney used to be. The outer world has intruded all too successfully into our silences and secrets.

Look for no odysseys of the imagination in four hundred weekly words of journalism. (Poetry with its rhythms, symbols, patterns, takes no harm from brevity.) These 'Letters from Hamnavoe' are walks out of doors in all weathers. You meet this neighbour, that friend, and linger and gossip a little about the weather and the old days; drop into a shop for tobacco, maybe; look over a garden wall at green things growing. The sound of the sea is everywhere.

You notice a new structure that must have something to do with oil in Scapa Flow. Then it is time to stroll home again, wondering mildly if the yeast has 'taken' in the bin of new ale. Such a brief, quiet perambulation is the typical 'Letter From Hamnavoe'.

Since this book would not have seen the light but for the enthusiasm and persistence of Brian Murray, that lover of literature and ancient stones and all things Orcadian, I dedicate it to him, in friendship.

G. M. B.

The First Letter

18.2.1971

It is proposed each week to write a letter to some Stromness 'exile' in Auckland or Vancouver or the Falkland Islands (or anywhere else) letting him know some of the things they are saying along Victoria Street and Franklin Road.

It is a queer time, when you think of it, to begin letter-writing, because the postmen have been on strike for a month now, and this is almost certainly the only letter being written in Stromness today.

We miss the postmen grievously—we never really appreciated them till now. Every morning regularly I was awakened by the rattle of the letterbox and the whispering fall of letters on the lobby floor; and that more than the thought of breakfast made me get out of bed. It might only of course be the hydro-electric bill, or the *Time-Life* offer of some superb book that would transform my whole life...

And then again, in the afternoon, what took my feet homeward from the piers or the west shore but the expectation of a scattering of white rectangles on the lobby floor; I lifted them up with a leaping of the heart...

And even to see the postmen going their rounds with their blue uniforms and heavy bags was a comforting and reassuring thing—the letterboxes rattling in sequence up Hillside Road and round the Ness housing schemes.

We Orcadians feel very isolated these days as one of the most precious things in life, the communication between friends, has dried up.

Measured for Europe

25.2.1971

They are softening us up to become Europeans in a few years time. First it was Centigrade instead of Fahrenheit. Last week it was decimal currency. Soon—they say—it'll be metres instead of feet or yards, and when you go in for a drink you'll have to ask for a litre of beer, please.

They say Decimal Day went smoothly on the whole, but there were more than a few old bodies in the shops of Hamnavoe who fumbled about in their purses and didn't know whether they were standing on their heads or their heels. And, said one old lady, 'Couldn't they have waited until all us old folk were dead?'

We still have ha'pennies and pennies, though. They don't seem to be much good to the kids nowadays, even with their higher value; but when you and I got a penny on a Saturday we wouldn't have called the king our cousin; standing and lingering about two or three shop windows along the street, from Janetta Sinclair's to old Ma Cooper's, before deciding on a liquorice strap, a lucky bag, a bar of Highland Cream toffee or a sherbet dab.

And that marvellous coin, the sixpence, they say is marked for early extinction.

(Of course: how could a two-and-a-half-new-pence coin endure for very long!) With the old prewar sixpence you could, if you were a sweetie-loving boy, buy up nearly all the confectionery in Stromness and still have twopence left over for *The Wizard*.

Decimalisation everywhere, as we get measured for Europe. But, curiously enough, there are some areas into which, it seems, the reformers dare not intrude. Time, for example. I have never heard it suggested yet that the day should be split into ten hours and every hour into ten minutes, and every minute into ten seconds. But if you live till the year 2000 you might find it so.

Place names

Wednesday isn't going to be the same in Stromness from now on. It was always the most stirring day of the week here, with the farmers coming into the mart and their wives shopping here and there along the street; and in the afternoon a fine mingling of folk about the Pier Head, fishermen and farmers and dockers and seamen. From last Wednesday on, the North Boat (the weekly shiprun between Aberdeen and Stromness) stopped calling at Stromness: it is a lamentable subtraction from the trade and energy of the town. A little bleakness has settled on the middle of the week.

* * *

I supposed others than myself were surprised that the Town Council finally chose the name Faravel for the new housing scheme on the side of the hill between Hoymansquoy and Mayburn. If I remember rightly, the name was said to have been found on some old map. Alas, old maps are notoriously unreliable—in the good old days, with place names, anything went. Some ignorant mapmaker is to blame, no doubt, because we now call our island capital Kirkwall instead of Kirkvoe (which is a much lovelier name, besides, of course, being accurate).

Another Scottish pedant in the sixteenth century tried to saddle the main island of our group with the ludicrous name Pomona!—which nobody, I'm glad to say, ever calls it nowadays. (We would not, however, have the name of that fine tavern, the Pomona Inn, in Finstown changed, for now it is deeply rooted in the affections of everyone in the west.)

Of course what our ancestors settled for in the end, the name Mainland, is entirely colourless, and one uses it without any relish at all. For the Norsemen this island was Hrossey, 'the horse island'. One hopes, rather forlornly I must admit, that in the next generation or two that beautiful name will slowly gain currency again.

To return to Faravel. Not many people, I imagine, will dispute with the late Dr Hugh Marwick about Orkney place names. This is what he has to say, in *Birsay Place Names*, about the name Farafield: 'Origin uncertain but discussed in OFN (*Orkney Farm Names*). Possibly an ON[1] *vartha-fjall*, "beacon hill"...'

If that is so, then the hill on which our new housing scheme stands has its summit at 'the Look-out' or 'the Gun'. There the fires were lit to warn the people that a hostile fleet was approaching; and more joyously, for the midsummer fire festivals.

The Kirks United

18.3.1971

Well, it seems to be over at last, the generations-long Presbyterian schism in Stromness. Of course, officially it came to an end in 1929, when the Church of Scotland became one again after nearly two centuries of splitting up into sects and factions. I was never able to unravel them in my mind; but if ever I was in doubt I went to Peter Esson's[2] tailor shop at the foot of Church Road. Peter Esson had a fine detailed enthusiastic knowledge of the history of Presbyterianism in Scotland; and of the flowering and fading of the Seceders, the Burghers, the Antiburghers, the Relief, the Cameronians, and of course the Free Kirk that hived off at the Disruption of 1843. Peter was a son of that Free Kirk, if ever there was one. He had been christened 'Peter Learmonth' after the first Free Kirk minister in Stromness; his mother, I think, had been a servant in Rev Peter Learmonth's manse...

Officially the Church of Scotland became one in 1929, but in the peedie[3] town of Stromness there continued to be three ministers and three congregations—the Owld Kirk, the Free Kirk and the UP Kirk—and they held fiercely to their independence. I suppose if you have sat in the same family pew since childhood, and your forebears

---

1 Orkney Norn—Dictionary of the old Norn tongue that was still being spoken in parts of Orkney in the eighteenth century—*The Orkney Norn*, by Hugh Marwick (Oxford UP, 1929).

2 See 'The Death of Peter Esson, Tailor, Librarian, Free Kirk Elder' (*Loaves & Fishes*—Hogarth, 1959).

3 peedie (the Orkney Norn), small.

before that, and your remote ancestors carried stones on their backs from the quarry to the building of the church, a certain loyalty is inbred...

But now, at last, they have all agreed to come together in the old UP Kirk in Victoria Street (where I have sat in the highest seat in the gallery with all the douce sweetie-eating family in the days of childhood; and especially I remember the long sermons on summer Sunday afternoons, when the bluebottles were droning in the windows...).

But poor Peter Esson, how sorry I would have been for him if he had been alive—for it was the North Church that he loved with his whole heart, every stone and joist of it—and I think this union (though obviously necessary and welcome in a hundred ways) might well have broken his heart.

The Bus

25.3.1971

There must be a sizeable number of Orcadians who have never been inside a bus for years; because it is so much more convenient to go to kirk or market in your own car. And yet a leisurely bus trip on a spring day can be delightful, between Stromness and Kirkwall. Cheap too, as things go nowadays—it is only five bob (or 25 new pence) return, whereas in prewar days it was three-and-six, a small fortune; but of course well worth it to see the County Show or the Orkney v Shetland football match.

The bus starts, then, from the Pier Head, with its few passengers and parcels; the driver-conductor having previously collected the fares. A few shivering folk get on near the War Memorial. (It is a very cold spring morning I am talking about, the coldest day of the year up to now; for the winter was like winter in Tunis or Mexico). The bus ambles on. Will it rain? There is a predominant grey in the sky. The strong north wind has kept the *St Ola* harbour-fast. A few swans go, superbly, over the gurls on Stenness Loch.

It will not rain—only snow could issue from that glower of sky in the north. A few farm women get on. The bus saunters past the drained green moorland between Stenness and Harray, and sylvan Binscarth (a cluster of dry sticks still in the valley above the Oyce) and stops of course once or twice in Finstown... (How remiss—I forgot to mention the most famous building in Orkney after the cathedral—The Golden Slipper, a famous tea-house and meeting place at the Brig-o-Waithe; it is, alas, roofless now, lying far behind between the loch and the tip of the Bay of Ireland)... Finstown has a skirt of fine new bungalows now: isn't it a wonder they don't build their houses higher on the side of the beautiful Hill of Heddie?...

A web of silvery wires lies delicately across the upper flank of Wideford. The morning is definitely brightening. And isn't it a wonder they don't drive the main road, as in pre-1939 days, straight along the shore into Kirkwall, instead of having that wide insipid loop round Hatston?

Down the brae of Hatston the bus trundles doucely, with its few farmers and farmers' wives. There are the boats, and St Magnus like a huge Rhode Island Red that gathers her chickens (the homes of Kirkwall) under her wing. And why—to ask one more question before we turn into Junction Road—why are Kirkwallians so furtive about the Peerie Sea, when it could be made a marvellous asset to the town?... It will not snow; indeed a little wan sunlight is falling over the roofs of Kirkwall. The bus stops. I get out.

I hope, dear Orkneyman in a distant place, that you won't mind being put in mind (what a clumsy piece of writing!) of the pleasures of a 45-minute bus trip between the two towns—which you must have done many a time in the old days.

An Empty Kirk

1.4.1971

What will happen to the North Church, soon to stand empty in the middle of the town? No doubt the arbiter's reasons for choosing St Peter's-Victoria Street were cogent, but still the North Church remains the more aesthetically satisfying of the two. The tall slender steeple, seen from the piers, breaks the skyline well; certainly the architect at the turn of the century knew exactly where to place it, among all that tumult of roofs. It is no less beautiful viewed from the back of the town. Perhaps from the summit of Brinkie's Brae it looks best of all.

Stromness would certainly be an uglier place without that fine steeple, and most Stromnessians hope that there will be no thought of pulling it down.

And what of the building itself? Will Stromness at last get the theatre and concert hall that it has sorely lacked for a long time? Would the North Church do for a town hall?—for certainly our present town hall is an eyesore that grows no mellower with the years.

You hear people saying that the North Church is awkwardly placed, surrounded with steps and behind a warren of closes. But even so, its situation is in keeping with all the rest of the town: what is Stromness but a tumbling stone wave, a network of closes, a marvel of steps from the seaweed up to the granite of Brinkie's Brae...

The North Church fits beautifully into the scheme; and all loyal Stromnessians must hope that a good deal of imagination will be put, within the next few months, into the disposal of this building, which is one of the town's undoubted assets.

A Trip to Edinburgh

15.4.1971

A few days in the south is a good tonic at this time of year, after a winter of hard work. (In a way it was another piece of work I had to do, as one of two judges in the students' verse competition held annually by BBC radio, but so small and pleasant that it was part of the enjoyment.) I always have qualms about flying, but once the plane is up and over the Pentland Skerries I feel as free and secure as a seabird; only the landing at Wick is a bit of a nuisance, for the airport there is not a place of beauty. At Aberdeen (Dyce) you can stretch your legs, have a glass of beer and a small cigar, before handing back your yellow boarding card at the hole in the side of the plane to the polite steward; and a few minutes after that you see the two Forth bridges gleaming below, and Turnhouse comes tilting and looming up at you, and the plane bumps gently to a halt. You half expect a car and a familiar face, and sit for a while over coffee and a sandwich in the airport cafe before catching a bus into Princes Street. The old familiar tavern in Rose Street is full of new faces—yes, and the old beery tables have been removed and oak beams put across the dark smoky ceiling, and the place is full of young barmaids (all the faithful old retainers, except one, are gone). What still remains are the photographs of Scotland's poets—a gey mixture—along the walls. So, among all these strangers, I sigh and down my pint of export, and grasp my single piece of baggage, and wait for the bus in the cold darkening air outside... The next afternoon, waiting to do the first part of my small pleasurable job of work at the BBC, I sat in the Gardens and watched the latest fashions going past: young girls wearing midi-coats, which gave to all that springtime litheness an old-fashioned trollopy look; yet wear them they must, it seems, when some fashion prince in Paris or London cracks the whip. Then I wandered over the hill and along Queen Street to the BBC... But that is another story and I have come to the end of my writing paper.

A Poet Discovered

29.4.1971

It was over at last, all my business in Edinburgh. For an hour or so a group of us had sat in the silent submarine light of a BBC studio in Edinburgh, discussing poetry. The students of Scotland had sent in their essays in this most difficult of arts, and we had sifted through them all winter to discover the wheat. It was a joy to recognise, here and there, a marvellous talent. So the winning verses were read, and the comments made, and the winner (a girl student art teacher[1] from Glasgow) interviewed; while behind a wide glass panel the studio

1 Liz Lochhead

16

managers worked their dials and switches. At last the tension was broken—the half hour was up—everybody looked at each other and smiled. Another recording was in the can.

A day or two later I took a Sunday morning train from Waverley, and we rattled and swayed on that urgent powerful rhythm through the ports and farmlands and industrial towns of Fife. At Dundee (the train went no further) my friends, Peter and Betty Grant from Aberdeen, were waiting for me. The car nosed cautiously through the renovated heart of Dundee and out into the country. After a week of high and remote serenity, the clouds had descended once more; there was a haze on the fields, a rawness, a threat of rain. At the side of a high lonely Perthshire road we had a picnic in the car—sandwiches and chocolate cake and coffee out of a thermos. In the high skiing country there were only scars of snow after this mildest of winters, but still a few hopeful sportsmen on their great awkward wooden feet plodded from snowfield to snowfield...

In Aberdeenshire the heavens opened and the rain descended. Balmoral was only a turret among whispering dripping trees. We followed the course of the hidden Dee towards Aberdeen. The granite in the rain was a deeper grey than ever. Home at last, we had a marvellous dinner and a bottle of wine, and a great deal of talk, and before bedtime a jar of Guinness.

Aberdeen

6.5.1971

In the car one afternoon, Peter and I drove a big swathe through Aberdeenshire and Banffshire. But first we spent twenty minutes or so in Torry, now of course part of the big city, but still bearing the marks of its original sea-thirled independence. And another half-hour or so in Old Aberdeen, a fragrant and gracious place which is gathering into itself all the new university buildings—it will be again, as it was once, the precinct of the gown.

Then we made for the countryside and the coast, in a grey but acceptable spring air. We passed through towns I had never seen—

Peterhead, Fraserburgh—but then Peter took me to two incredible villages hanging cheek by jowl on to the steep Banffshire cliffs. Slowly the car slanted down the steepest road in Scotland; it hung over roofs and rocks; and we found ourselves in Crovie. The single line of cottages—all fishermen's originally, but now, they say, the well-off folk are buying up the places for summer cottages—is built under formidable buttresses of cliff. The main street is a narrow ribbon between the gable ends and the sea; it will never have a single car going through it. It seems a dangerous enchanting little place.

Its sister village, Gardenstown, is a mile or so round the coast. It is bigger, and a bit more complex, being built on four or five levels from the cliff top to the sea edge. It has a kirk, hotel, shops. It is said to be a leading stronghold of the Close Brethren. It is one of the strangest places in Scotland, a tribute to men (who will go anywhere and try anything in search of a livelihood) in their struggle with the vertical.

We came home via Macduff and Turriff.

I wandered next afternoon into the Art Gallery, and saw an exhibition of Benno Schotz the sculptor; and next door, a Lewis Grassic Gibbon exhibition. Great interest has been aroused in Aberdeenshire and the Mearns by the series of plays on BBC2 by this local author of *Sunset Song*. There were his school exercise books, and a replica of a farm kitchen of the early twentieth century, and stills from the film, etc.

My stay in Aberdeen was all too short and hurried—my apologies to all friends I couldn't get visiting this time—I hope to see them later in the summer, perhaps.

Next morning I sat at Dyce waiting for an hour-late plane from Edinburgh. It was delayed because of fog further south. We embarked; the plane took its first great leap over the Moray Firth. At Wick the clouds were shredding out, and the sky showed patches of blue. Half-way in the short hop over the Pentland Firth the sun came dazzling in, and in Orkney it was a beautiful warm day.

Blots

13.5.1971

I am not disturbed by the *Northolmen*[1] lying under the churchyard, and I don't think many other Stromness folk are either. There is something symbolic in the juxtaposition of wreck and tombstones. More than one visitor has told me how impressed he was by the sheer drama of it. The *Northolmen* has been there for four and a half years now. Salt and rust are gnawing at it all the time. There may come a day when it will be leprous and unsightly and insanitary, and then perhaps what is left will have to be carted off. But not, I think, for a few years yet.

What is disturbing when one walks round the coast is the sight of that half-demolished tower and those searchlight emplacements from the Second World War. They were never things of beauty, even in their pristine state, but over the years the Stromness folk had come to accept them. The local fishermen found the high tower at Links Battery a useful landmark. Boys played imaginative games in it. It may have been a lover's meeting place. A couple of summers ago there were loud explosions to the west of the town—we were told that the army was demolishing what it had itself erected between 1939 and 1942. But when we took a stroll round the shore to see the landscape as it had been in the time of its innocence, we got a rude shock. The demolition, at least from the point of view of Stromnessians, had not been successful. The tower was a heap of hideous rubble. The searchlight emplacements showed a few small scorched holes, but were otherwise intact, except that they were uglier than they had been before the attempt was made.

These scabs are liable to outlast the *Northolmen*, for concrete is notoriously obdurate stuff.

Another blot on the landscape is the dump[2] as you approach the town. It reeks and stinks there, right beside the Kirkwall road. It is very doubtful if the hundred thousand tourists who are said to be coming to Orkney in future summers will be enchanted by it, at all.

---

1 A Norwegian fishing boat wrecked in Hoy Sound in 1966.
2 The dump has now been removed.

Exhibition

27.5.1971

There's a particularly good exhibition on at the Museum just now. I have been twice to see it and I hope to see it a few times yet before the end of the summer. It will be fascinating for local folk as well as for visitors, for it is about the Stromness of our grandfathers and great-grandfathers. The photograph section is beautifully presented —it shows the town at the end of last century, close by close, from the South End to the North End.

Stromness looks of course very much the same now as it did then, only for the houses that have here and there been knocked down, notably in Graham Place. But what connection is there between the healthy well-dressed children of 1971 and those peaked anonymous barefoot bairns of 1890? The latter are the grandparents of the former. There has certainly in the meantime been a great advance in our material standards, due in part to men like Keir Hardie and the 'red gospellers' of Clydeside.

The photographs—all reproduced and mounted from old albums and private collections by Mr Wilfred Marr—are fascinating, but they form only one part of the exhibition. Every aspect of old Stromness is displayed in the cases: Gow the pirate (with the rare books on him by Defoe and Scott); the Kirk (with photos of the old horse-and-cart picnics to Swanbister, and communion tokens, etc); education, showing the peedie schools, for example Samuel Hourston's at the top of Hellihole, and a book of melancholy verses by a schoolmistress, Cecilia Hourston; Local Government, including stern warnings from the Town Clerk of 1902 that the Stromness folk must by law put running water and water closets into their houses; the West Shore, with kelp-burning and such wrecks and heroic rescues as the *Shakespeare* and the *Carmenia II*; and a Drinking and Smoking section which shows the old Distillery and distillery workers where Mayburn now is, and also a genuine bottle (unopened) of 'Old Orkney' whisky, together with advertisement posters and mirrors of the same—and a dram glass from The White Horse Inn at the North End—and old porcelain tobacco pipes that the more prosperous skippers and merchants smoked.

To the two Stromness men, Bryce Wilson and John Pottinger, who planned and set up the Exhibition with such skill, many congratulations.

The Gentle Tap

3.6.1971

All through a year things have been happening at Ness, apart of course from the boat-building and the golf. A major sports complex is nearing completion, with new tennis court and bowling green. Dominating it will be a modern social club where all the sports folk of Stromness will foregather for talk and refreshment, after the racquets have been put away, and the bowls are back in the box, and the 19th-hole thirst takes over.

It looks as if it will be a pleasant place on a summer evening.

But to achieve all this, a rare thing has had to be sacrificed. I refer to Stromness's world-famous putting green. It was an absolutely unique 18-hole course. The top half of it was level enough; the lower half was a system of little hills and valleys, and you had to be a very good putter indeed to master it. It required perfect co-ordination of hand and eye. Otherwise your subtle stroke might end among the bluebells; or, if it hadn't rained for a week and the grass was newly shaven, you might spend half an hour trying to hole out on the flank of a little hill—it was the torture of Sisyphus; for unless you were dead accurate, the ball curved round the hole and came back to your feet, time after maddening time.

On a prewar summer afternoon the putting green was occupied by a group of elderly gentlemen, who spiced their play with solemn banter and sallies of reminiscence.

Among those who played regularly were Jimmy Bruce the postman, Captain Sinclair of Whitehouse, William Robertson of Hellihole, Rev Thomson the Episcopal minister, William Spence the baker, and my father (who brought me along with him: I was useful for taking the balls out of the holes and seeing to the pins). What jubilation among those ancients if one of them chanced to hole in one! What bitterness if one of them stymied the other! What stories, when the game was over and they sat smoking their pipes on the green bench outside the Golf House! So it went on all the summer afternoon—the gentle tap of putter on ball, the cries of delight and amazement and frustration until tea-time sent them home over Ness Road.

I have a tremulous hope—I do not really know, for I have asked no one—that there may still be enough ground left over, next the sea road, for a small putting green, once tennis court and bowling green are finished. Even nine holes would be better than nothing.

The Menace of Cars

10.6.1971

Some time it will have to stop, or life in Stromness will become impossible. You walk through the street some days, and are caught in a maelstrom of cars. The worst times are Wednesday afternoon and Saturday afternoon, though Friday afternoon isn't a long kick behind. What is worrying is that pedestrians are relegated to some inferior kind of animal, a pest in the way of those new lords of the road. No doubt of it, put some otherwise gentle respectable folk in drivers' seats and all their innate aggressiveness and rudeness come boiling to the surface. But even if these knights of the road were courtesy and consideration itself—and doubtless most of them are, still—the proliferation of cars is a serious thing in a place like Stromness. The men who built our town knew nothing faster than the horse. And they weren't too keen on having many of them about the place; in Porteous's Brae in Dundas Street there were steps where only pedestrians could go. At the turn of the century, the Town Council forbade bicycles on the street until they were challenged in the High Court and defeated. It seems laughable to us now, but it is just possible that the instinct of the Council was right. Did they perhaps foresee the nuisance that progress was about to unleash on our streets?

We are told that the numbers of cars on our roads will multiply frighteningly in the next decade or two. In the last ten years it has become increasingly difficult for a pedestrian to walk in peace from the South End to the North End. I have a vivid impression that this June is worse than last June. And all this before the summer visitors stream across the Pentland Firth, bringing their cars with them in thousands.

This will be put down to the moan of a reactionary pedestrian. I admit it comes out of selfishness, in part. But I also think there is a danger of our society choking 'in its own too much'.

First Tourists

17.6.1971

This month isn't like last June at all, all aflame with warmth and colour from beginning to end. The wind has lain in the east for weeks; sometimes it shifts about a point or two north or south, but east is the predominant airt; and the east wind is a siccar wind in Orkney.

So everybody is going about, day after day, shivering a little, and wondering if it was wise to shift into thin summer clothes at the end of May. A sea haar lingered about for days. One day the sky opened and it rained tumultuously. But every now and again there are those small gleams of June light, a fracture of blue among the grey clouds, that is reflected in the sea; and among all the coldness and austerity of this June we must marvel again at such beauty. And for a few days past there have been consolations: however grey and overcast the day, in late evening the ruck of cloud moves away and then the old June magic is everywhere in sea and sky, and the summer glow never leaves the north.

The visitors are beginning to come now. You see them everywhere in the street: a great number of them young folk with rucksacks on their backs and faces brown as gipsies. It may be that these young students from all over Europe do nothing much to boost our tourist trade, and look as if they could live happily on mugs of tea, eggs, bread and margarine—but I always like to see them around, for it seems to me that they are enjoying themselves in the way that Orkney should be enjoyed... And by the way, isn't it time that there were hostels for these young wayfarers in Kirkwall and Stromness?[1]

I must say I like to see all the new faces on our streets in the summer.

Some local folk are worried that Orkney might come to depend too much on tourism; but the kind of visitors we get are not looking for amusement arcades and the 'instant joy' of a holiday camp. I like to think they come for what Orkney can truly give them: 'the dearest freshness deep down things...'

Progress

24.6.1971

Go for a walk among the fields or along the shore nowadays, and as like as not you will hear a tinny music approaching—a teenager with a transistor. You pass by, your teeth on edge. It is made all the worse because the teenager doesn't appear to be listening to his portable music; and of course the sound of the seabirds and the waves must be utterly blocked out for him. Portable transistors are one of the very worst inventions of our time.

And yet we of the old brigade were there when it all began. I remember sitting in a house trying to hear, with earphones, a Scotland-England football commentary. It must have been about 1932. All the boys were football-daft then too. All that came through was a tantalising whisper, that sometimes faded away into utter silence. Yet we experienced the excitement of Wembley that Saturday afternoon. 'What a wonderful thing the wireless is!' we said to each other; although Scotland, if I remember rightly, lost 3-0.

A gramophone was borne into our house one day. It had a horn. There was a tin of needles and a few heavy black discs. The needle was set to the revolving disc, and behold, a mystery! A pawky, merry Scottish voice sang 'Doctor MacGregor and his wee black bag'... Another disc, and a hillbilly voice gave a tender nasal farewell to his sweetheart,

1 There are now.

'Remember the Red River Valley, and the cowboy that loved you so true'... Another disc, and a voice of angelic purity soared: 'O for the wings of a dove'...

The gramophone was another great triumph for the scientists. A new priesthood had been firmly established on earth. We hailed each one of their marvels. Most of us still do not doubt that, in spite of everything, they have the solution to all our problems. To them boundless faith and reverence are accorded.

In these lovely midsummer evenings, walking along the Nethertoon shore road, one thinks with horror that some day soon a tanker might excrete its oil somewhere off Hoy, and the tide and the wind might bear a ten-mile-deep slick to this beautiful shore.

Street Scars

1.7.1971

We must be very grateful to our forefathers who built Stromness. They were supposed to be ignorant, inartistic men, yet over the generations, each man building for himself, they produced this harmony. We must assume that these men were not concerned in the slightest with art and beauty—people only think of these sophistications when they have leisure and money. The makers of Stromness were merchants and seamen and fishermen, their lives hard graft from childhood to old age. Perhaps to build functionally—as they had to do—is to build beautifully.

Summer visitors are pleased, among other things, with our street of flagstone that meanders this way and that, and surges up and down like a wave. It is the flagstones that make it so lovely. Why, they wonder, do the flagstones give out in mid-Victoria Street, to be replaced, northwards, by those uniform concrete squares? Why, indeed?

There must still be quarries somewhere in the West Mainland that could yield flagstones to give us back our original street.

These concrete squares, the more one lives with them, become uglier. Most of the materials that men work in mellow with age: wood, stone, metal. But time is not in love with concrete: after one smart slick month it begins to crumble and wither.

The street southward from the Manse Lane is still flagstone, except for ominous small patches of concrete here and there. What seems to be happening is that wherever a flagstone gets worn and broken—and with those great vehicles that thunder through our street, what else can happen?—when a flagstone gives out, it is replaced by one of those sickly looking concrete squares: and it is as if the street were scabbed with some strange sickness.

I hope the Stromness members of the Heritage Society will keep an eye firmly on the situation.

Summer Holidays

8.7.1971

There are children swarming everywhere in the sunshine—down piers, up closes—at all hours, because it is the summer holidays.

I wonder if they have the same glorious feeling of freedom that we had, a generation ago, when the summer holidays came. School was more of a bore in those days, we were more 'cribbed, cabined, confined'. Such things as parsing, analysis, vulgar fractions, soured our young souls. When the first sunny days of June came, we began to hope that these things would not go on for ever: the seaports of France, the Stuart dynasty, 'There's a breathless hush in the close tonight...'

The days grew longer and warmer and the bag of books hung heavier at our shoulders. At last the miraculous morning of deliverance came. We handed back our school books. There was an air of kindliness and friendliness everywhere in the classroom. Our nice teacher gave all the fifty of us a penny each (and you could buy two lucky bags for a penny in those days). When the school bell rang at one o'clock the playground was one wild outburst of joy.

The summer holidays was a Saturday that went on for eight weeks. To a small child eight weeks is a joyous eternity. We did what I'm sure Stromness children did a hundred years ago and will still be doing in the twenty-first century. We fished for sillocks at the end of piers. We chased butterflies across Brinkie's Brae. We 'dipped' at the Tender Tables and Warbeth, and had picnics, with sand in the sandwiches and flies in the tea. On one special day we went in the bus to Kirkwall. We rowed about in the harbour. We played football till darkness fell.

The only real difference is that we ran through these hot summers in bare feet, being much poorer than modern children. We did not know we were poor. The spendthrift sun dowered us with all the wealth we wanted.

Rousay

15.7.1971

One of the pleasant things about summer is that you can make a day's jaunt here or there.

Last Friday a few of us decided to go to Rousay. It was a lovely morning: sun, high white clouds, pleasantly warm. At Tingwall jetty workmen were busy extending the pier. A huge lorry arrived from Kirkwall loaded with bags of cement. On the beach a young seal dragged itself here and there. For some reason it had left the sea. It was being kept alive with milk. The workmen did not think it would live long.

Wyre, Eynhallow, Egilsay. At Rousay pier a Landrover was waiting to take us to a field near the mill and Suso Burn where the Boys' Brigade from Stromness had pitched their camp. They had had a week of mostly good weather. They gave us a marvellous lunch of liver and potatoes, then fruit salad; and you wouldn't have got such service and courtesy in the best hotel.

In the afternoon we went in the Landrover round the island's circular road, in quest of a cottage. A threatened rain haze dispersed. We climbed up the magnificent Kierfea road. Far below the sea stretched and whitened. We admired the sprawl of Westray to the north. The hillside seemed to be alive with rabbits.

We came down into Wasbister and climbed slowly again into the most beautiful fringe of Rousay—Westness with its golf course and prehistoric monuments. It was sad to think that this was once the most populous and prosperous part of the island, until a clearance last century replaced the 'bold peasantry' with sheep.

We were very kindly received by Mrs Firth of Westness, who showed us one or two possible cottages on the west side of the island. Some of the Stromness boys were helping a farmer in his hayfield. It was time to get back to the ferry. Once more in the camp canteen we got a marvellous meal of corned beef and tomatoes and tea. The tide was far out. Mansie Flaws the ferryman had to carry the children down the ladder into the boat.

At Tingwall the poor sick seal still sprawled on the stones. We had not found an entirely suitable cottage—a lonely set-apart primitive place near the sea, suitable for the making of music—but, to use an Orkney understatement, we had had a good enough day.

Good Weather

22.7.1971

I am writing this on the eve of Shopping Week[1]. Everyone is hoping for good weather. The past week has not been good; cold, grey, north-east winds, frequent rain. The Stromnessians are convinced that the sun is saving up all its warmth and light to squander in the next seven days. By the time you read this you will know for sure if Shopping Week 1971 is sun-splashed or rain-soaked. (Most likely it will be a mixture of the two, with a neutral day here and there.)

A lot depends on what weather you consider 'good'. People have queer ideas about the weather. I walked round the shore on a conventionally 'bad' afternoon this past week. There was half a gale blowing from the northwest and I had to shelter in the lee of the old lifeboat shed from a sudden wild blatter of rain. Yet it was the best walk I have had for a

1 Stromness's annual week of carnival in mid-July, organised by the Chamber of Commerce.

long time, under that tattered sky of white and grey and blue, leaning into the wind. And the Coolags of Hoy shrouded in rain, and the Ward Hill brilliant with sunlight. 'Stormy day,' an English visitor with a wife and two dogs called to me as he passed on the road. Yes, and exhilarating, and gay, and very, very good.

What exactly do you call a 'good' day? London and the south of England have been baking in temperatures up in the eighties. I can imagine few things more horrible than being cooped up in a great city in such conditions. I have had letters this past week that yearned for the cold, hard light of the north.

Yet that bakehouse weather is generally called 'good'.

I remember the last big snowfall in Orkney, in the January (or maybe the February) of 1969. The whiteness came in one wild abandoned abundance about breakfast-time one morning. In one hour the islands were transfigured. Stromness was an enchanted place, all crystal and swansdown and sapphire. It was a joy to walk through the heaped, hushed street. And yet nearly everybody you met said: 'What terrible weather!'

Something rather strange has happened to our sense of values.

Yet for this Shopping Week, I admit that what we want is sun, and warmth, and blue skies.

Carnival

29.7.1971

Well, the gods have been kind to Stromness this week. They have showered sunshine on the town from Monday to Friday. I am writing this on the Saturday and it is dull and wet. But now and then a little silver mixes with the pewter of the sky and gives one a hope that it will keep dry for the fancy dress parade in the evening.

I think there have never been such crowds in Stromness as this past week, not even on an old-time Stromness market day. What is surprising is the great numbers of young folk (but this may only be a symptom that one is growing old). Anyway, all that young blood has added to the gaiety and joy of the week. Guitars and long hair everywhere, and I must say this new generation strikes me as being a much healthier and happier breed than my own generation, which in spite of its virtues was poor and more anxious about things: and there was thirty years ago a tension between the sexes which does not appear to exist at all nowadays; and a good thing too.

'Shopping Week rolls on' proclaims the official programme in large red type, and indeed it is quite an achievement that this week of carnival has gone on flourishing now for twenty-two years. The great danger that it must always face is repetitiveness, the getting into ruts, boredom. So far the Shopping Week officials have skilfully avoided this by a continuous infusion of new energy and new ideas; such as the barbecue on the side of Brinkie's Brae (an outstanding success, this), and 'It's a Knock-Out', and the freefall parachute drop. For a few years past there was that lively revue in the Community Centre, in which the young folk of the town, with wit and verve and sauciness, cut their self-important elders down to size; what happened to that staged revelry this year? I'm sure we all missed it.

There may be other things worth keeping in mind for the future. A visitor from the south said to me, 'What a pity that more use is not made of the wonderful street here...' And he went on to say that some kind of local pageantry or play-cycle might well be a striking annual open-air event, a rich mingling of colour and music and history. The weather of course is always the uncertain element in an ambitious project like this, but now, even if it did rain, there is the spacious North Church available to hold performers and public.

The Pirate in the Classroom

5.8.1971

Two and a half centuries ago a boy walked along what is now called Garson's Shore towards the village of Stromness, or Cairston, or Hamnavoe (in those days, it seems, you could call that scatter of sea-bleached houses any one of the three). Where was he going? He was probably going to one of the small private schools in the village to learn how to read and spell and cipher: also perhaps a little Latin or French. The boy's father was one of the merchants of the port and therefore, along with some of the other merchants, he would have been able to employ a dominie to instruct his son.

So the boy sits in a dark room, along with maybe seven or eight other boys, and in the old furious Scottish tradition the wisdom of the world is shouted and beaten into him. Often the boy looks through the tall window at the harbour, and the ships of France and Norway and America anchored in the Cairston Roads.

It is interesting, in view of the dark and melodramatic ending of this boy's life, to speculate on his early behaviour. Would John Gow[1] have been a wild lad, always fighting with the other boys, playing truant down the piers, robbing birds' nests at Ernefea and Mooseland?

I do not think so. I see a lonely, withdrawn boy, who behaves well in class (though he does not particularly like his lessons) and has little to do with his schoolmates when the class is dismissed in the afternoon. He loves to wander among the foreign masts in the harbour. He walks by himself along the shore. He is a 'loner'.

But there is something very strange about him. When he is rebuked in class for not knowing his Latin declension or a multiplication table, he stands there quietly; but surely the dominie has seen the sudden, dangerous flash stabbing from his eye. It is all over in a second. The boy veils with his eyelids the smoulder inside him. Meekly he sits down.

That same mad flash Captain Oliver Ferneau of the ship *Caroline* saw one night in the Mediterranean, between Tunis and Genoa. The good, kind old master could not understand it. What had gone wrong with John Gow, the quiet, well-educated Orkney sailor whom he had entrusted with the key of the arms chest? John Gow stood with his pistol at the head of the mutinous crew. The rage, envy, spite, hatred, greed, pride which he had mustered in his soul all his life, suddenly burst out. Before that night was done, Captain Ferneau and all the officers of the *Caroline* had been murdered.

1 John Gow, Stromness pirate, executed in London, 1725.

The cut-throats chose for their pirate skipper the young man who had so obligingly dished out the cutlasses and pistols to them. John Gow seemed superior to them all—still in his hour of triumph a lonely, dedicated, doomed soul.

The Wizard of the North

19.8.1971

As the poet Hugh MacDiarmid says in the current *Radio Times*, there is something pretty awful in the fact that we seem only able to whip up interest in a man and his work whenever he has some kind of anniversary or centenary. He was writing about the current spate of essays and radio and TV programmes on Sir Walter Scott.

I was never a great fan of 'the wizard of the north' myself, dating from our schooldays when we had to learn great chunks of *Ivanhoe* and *The Talisman* every week, and then undergo a 'viva voce' about them. That —it was only to be expected—gave us a scunner to Sir Walter.

Of course, being a patriotic Orkneyman, I considered it my duty to read *The Pirate*. This I did in my free time after school, but I must confess I didn't enjoy it. Some years later I tried again, thinking perhaps a more mature mind might relish it better. But it was no go. The only thing I really enjoy about the novel are the notes at the end.

And yet Scott had marvellous gifts as a poet. His verse romances are, for modern tastes, a bit too long, but he wrote some magical lyrics, 'Proud Maisie' and 'Look not thou on beauty's charming'...

The fault is entirely in myself. There must have been something very remarkable in the man whose work fired the imagination of all Europe.

I wish I had been there when, having climbed up 'a series of dirty and precipitous lanes'—possibly the Bank Lane and the lane at Sinclair's View—he finally knocked at the door of the 'Keeper of the Winds', Bessie Millie, and heard from these corpse-grey lips all about the pirate Gow, whom Bessie Millie must have seen in Stromness when she was a young lass and he was ripening for the gallows.

But Gow himself, for my money, remains a much more fascinating character than Scott's Captain Cleveland.

When we were young we were told that nature had hewed out a mighty profile of Sir Walter Scott on the stone of the Kame of Hoy. Some of my contemporaries said yes, it was there for all to see. But to be quite honest, I have contemplated that magnificent cliff a thousand times and have never once seen the slightest resemblance.

Summer Day

26.8.1971

Thursday was some day along the western seaboard of Orkney. The sun was turned full on, and Warbeth beach was littered with sunbathers and seabathers. Ponies trotted along the wet, firm sand among the happy shrieks and the sandcastles. The Atlantic occasionally gave a lazy heave and sent in a great glittering wave that collapsed on the sand in white-and-blue thunderous ruin. All Orkney was soaked in light and warmth. There was the faintest haze in the west, just above the horizon line.

I sat for an hour or more among the rocks between Nethertown and the Tender Tables, and there was not another living creature in sight. How hypnotic it is to watch the slow insurge of the tide: time is withdrawn; the behaviour of the encroaching sea is fascinating and unpredictable. A wave washes in far—it souses thoroughly and utterly a rock that has been dry and sun-warm for the last twelve hours; and then it draws back again into the smother and the welter. The tide is flooding in fast from the open Atlantic and filling all the little bays of Orkney. And you think, 'The next wave will drown the rock utterly.' ...Not so; the sea chooses instead to smash a little burning rockpool with a crab in it. It breaks open the glassy prison; the crab is free again in the immensities of the ocean. And you think, 'This higher rock where I am sitting will not be submerged for another hour.' ...As if to warn you of the sea's unpredictability, an immaculate blue wave arches in from another angle and strikes the base of the rock and your face is sprinkled with cold, thrilling drops.

Then, superbly, the *St Ola* turns into Hoy Sound.

We have had too few of these warm, bright days this summer: the air has come drifting in too much from east and north.

The evenings are drawing in. It is delightful to sip a pint of beer in the hotel sun-porch above the harbour, after such a golden day. Shadows gloom the Sound: colours are drained slowly from the land; the sea-haar thickens. It is a luminous summer night; everything is at peace. But there is a small rage and spite and vindictiveness and savagery abroad. As you pass out into the growing darkness the midges cluster about your face and neck and hands, a slow persistent smoulder. And in lamp-lit windows here and there the moths are birring softly.

The Crown Jewels of Island Literature

2.9.1971

The word has somehow got around that Orkney books are worth a lot of money. So people are tending more and more to hoard them all away in the hope that prices will climb even higher; and even then they will not sell them but pass them on as family heirlooms, with great-grandfather's harpoon from the Davis Straits and Auntie Jessie's spinning wheel.

Some Orkney books are valuable, right enough: *Kirkwall in the Orkneys*, *A Tour Through Orkney and Shetland*, Anderson's *Orkneyinga Saga* and maybe a score of others.

Most of them are valuable only in proportion to what a reader gets out of them.

I have a bookcase full of Orkney books but I do not collect Orkney books because they are Orkney books—I have them because I like them. I look forward to dip into them often in the coming winter. There are pages and chapters that I never tire of reading—the Night of Terror section from Allan Fea's *The Real Captain Cleveland* (the mutiny on board the *Caroline* led by John Gow the Orkneyman); the Wyre section of Edwin Muir's *Autobiography*; Eric Linklater's 'Kind Kitty' and 'The Three Poets'; John Firth's *Reminiscences of an Orkney*

Parish; the dialect lyrics of Robert Rendall; the mannered, marvellous seventeenth-century prose of Rev James Wallace; Hugh Marwick on the Orkney dialect and place names; the fine nature essays of Duncan J.Robertson; Bishop Robert Reid's sonorous prose anent the reorganisation of the chapter and services of the Cathedral of St Magnus the Martyr just before the Reformation; a host of stories out of the *Orkneyinga Saga*, such as the confrontation of the two Sweyns, that violent, death-laden Christmas in the Hall of Orphir and the tragic killing of Earl Rognvald the First in the seaweed of Papa Stronsay, ashes and blood on his white linen priest-coat, betrayed by the barking of his little dog...

With books like these at my elbow, what need of *Twenty-Four Hours* and *Tomorrow's World*? Yet I keep a television set in the corner too, to get news and opinion about this distracted world of today.

September the Third

9.9.1971

Almost before you are aware of it the summer is over, we are in September, the autumn equinox is hard upon us, and we go wheeling down into the storms, the snow, the darkness of winter. It was all over too soon, the season of peaches (I never ate so many—this summer they were delicious), herrings, new potatoes, lettuce. Only a few of the summer visitors are left, playing guitars a little forlornly among the beer bottles, tramping through the reeds and the waters looking for autumn birdflights.

I remember a September the third, thirty-two years ago, and the sombre voice of an ancient, disillusioned statesman telling us over the wireless that we were at war. It was a rather exciting day for the young folk. We could not understand why our elders looked so stricken, for of course we had no knowledge of the Somme and Passchendaele and the war that was to end all wars and the land fit for heroes: and they still bore the scars.

The days following were entirely delightful. We were let off school, just a few days after the new session had begun. But we were given work to do all the same. Lorries transported hordes of senior school children to Warbeth Beach and there among the sand dunes we filled hundreds and hundreds of sandbags. The weather was glorious: we were given free lemonade to drink. All day long the lorries went back and forth between Warbeth and Stromness carrying the swollen sandbags and the shrill-voiced labourers.

It must have been about September the 7th or 8th that there was a great headline in one newspaper—'Siegfried Line Pierced at Twelve Points', and we nodded and said to ourselves that it would soon be over after all. But our elders had heard the same nonsense in 1914 and they looked unconvinced.

It was only that winter, when the *Royal Oak* had been sunk in safe Scapa Flow and the first bombers came probing the defences, that it began to dawn on some of us that we were in for a long, terrible war.

Street Names

16.9.1971

This business of naming new places in Stromness is rousing more interest than ever before, and that is all to the good. In the old days— I mean twenty years ago—nobody seemed to care. The thing about 'Ferry Road' is that it is simple and plain and functional, a welcome change after the high romanticism of 'Faravel' and the urban stylishness of 'Mayburn Court'. I think in these matters we should keep our feet firmly on the ground; after all we are attaching a label which might well have to do for a couple of centuries.

On the whole, I think that in the past Stromness has been reasonably felicitous in the names it has bestowed on its streets and roads and housing schemes. One regrets that the Plainstones was ever absorbed into Victoria Street, and that Porteous's Brae on one side and Hutchison's Brae on the other should be parts of Dundas Street: wouldn't The Brae for this part of the town be a better name? The awful egotism of the Victorians has been stamped all over our thoroughfares: Alfred Street and John Street, besides the two already mentioned... It is pleasant, though, that the very centre of the town should celebrate the name of our greatest townsman, Alexander Graham[1].

There is a joker in every pack, and I suppose nobody now knows who gave the name of Khyber Pass to Garrioch's Close. I think it was a minor stroke of inspiration. (It will be of interest to Stromnessians far from home that the lower end of the Khyber Pass is now blocked off temporarily while the restoration of a house is going on; the hordes of Afghans have now at weekends to stream into the civilised parts by other routes: Leslie's Close, the Kirk Road...)

I regretted the loss of fine names like Well Park and Stanger's Park a few years ago, when all those schemes at Ness were given the blanket name of Guardhouse Park. But surely we did well to rediscover the name Hoymansquoy, which is a little poem in itself.

A thing that has puzzled me for a long time: who is the Brinkie[2] of Brinkie's Brae, and when was the name given? In the old maps it is called simply Ward Hill, and I rather wish it was still called that.

The First House of Hamnavoe

30.9.1971

William Clark and his wife Mareon put the thatch on their new house at the Cairston shore, and opened their door and waited. The country folk of Cairston and Quholm looked suspiciously at this hostelry. They didn't use it themselves; they kept their cheese and salt beef in their cupboards; their kirns were always seething with ale; their cuithes smoked in the chimney. They doubted very much that that uncan[3] man would go bankrupt within a year.

But after the equinox in September there was a gale from the west and there came one day a French vessel to the roadstead, and before

---

1 Alexander Graham freed Stromness, and at the same time all small burghs, from the commercial tyranny of the royal burghs; and he ruined himself financially by his efforts.

2 Some light perhaps is thrown on the name in future 'Letters'. See p177.

3 Stranger.

sunset a Spaniard. The queer-mouthed sailors came to Clark's Inn for chickens and fish and ale. There was some difficulty about the payment. William Clark did not trust the queer-like coins they offered him. There were whisperings and winks and handshakes down at the shore. William Clark settled for a cask of French wine and a large rum-smelling block of Virginian tobacco. The two skippers rowed out behind the Holms well pleased.

That winter Clark and his well-handed wife did a good trade.

Horsemen—officers about the business of Earl or Bishop— dismounted in the yard and tied up their horses and went into the dark fragrant bothy for a refreshment. It was not easy, riding between the Orphir hills, or all the way from the Barony of Birsay, on a bitter winter day.

When William Clark took the shutters from his window in the morning he would turn and look across the water of Hamnavoe to see if any ships had anchored there during the night. On the east side of the bay were the solid long-established farms: Garson, Hammigar. On the west side were only a few fishermen's bothies. William Clark doubted very much whether anything could be done with that sleep granite slope. But he knew he had done a good thing to build his inn where it was, because there was not a more sheltered harbour anywhere in Orkney.

When spring came a few of the younger farmers went to Clark's, half out of curiosity, half because they were tired and thirsty from the ploughing, and it was a better place for a singsong than a croft kitchen. The fishermen and the farmers and the sailors would sit at separate tables and not have much to say to each other. And once or twice a knife flashed, and the good wife screamed, and then William Clark came and stood between the fire-breathers and admonished them with sharp words.

This was the beginning of Stromness, when in the year 1580 a feu charter was granted to William Clark and his wife Mareon Chalmer 'with power of brewing and selling, keiping of ostelrie and bying of all thingis appertening thereto for furnissing of the commounes and utheris resorting thairaway'.

Where Is Santa Cruz?

7.10.1971

Lately—as some of you may have guessed—I have been interested in the pirate John Gow, that intriguing character who was hanged in London for his crimes in 1725.

He was a very bad man indeed—a plotter, inciter, murderer, robber—and yet there was some element in his nature that nowadays we call, for want of a more accurate word, 'charm'. It was this charm of his, this seeming openness and trustworthiness, that led the master of the *Caroline* to advance Gow from the crew to be his second mate. Another aspect of the famous charm made him the unanimous choice of the mutinous crew to be their leader, and later skipper, of the *Revenge* (as the *Caroline* was renamed). And again, when the peaceful, but powerfully armed *George* (which was the third name of the same ship, and a right true and leal and royal name it was, being the same as his then majesty the king) cast anchor in Cairston roads in the winter of 1724-25, there is plenty of evidence as to Gow's popularity with the local girls. There was an active love affair with a Miss Gordon, daughter of one of the chief citizens of the town. Furthermore, the scoundrel knew how to conduct himself socially; there were parties on board the *George* as well as in the best houses ashore.

Some of the black-avised, sleazy characters who went about everywhere with Gow must, all the same, have given rise to some speculation. 'Jack Gow, noo, he's done right weel at sea, aye has he, and gotten his own ship, but my mercy, what a lock o' villains he has for a crew.'

In such charisma as Gow possessed there is perhaps always a core of weakness. In the end Gow could not control the villains in his ship: they strangled hens, they stole tankards out of taverns, at the street corners they tested knives speculatively on their thumbs: and at last it got to be that the mothers of Hamnavoe wouldn't let their daughters over the door at night.

The object of writing the above is to ask readers where Santa Cruz is. Every self-respecting atlas lists about fifty towns called Santa Cruz. It was while sailing between Santa Cruz and Genoa that the mutiny occurred on the *Caroline*. This particular Santa Cruz, says Allan Fea, is in Northern Africa; and Tudor says the Barbary Coast. What I should be grateful to know is whether this phantom town is on the Mediterranean coast or the Atlantic coast[1].

The Lamplighter

14.10.1971

The bright lights are on in Stromness. For weeks past county council men, hoisted high in cages above lorries, have been fixing new powerful lamps all along the street as far as Ness Road. Now Stromness at night is all a white radiance, except for Cairston Road, which has been favoured with red sodium lamps. You never saw such brightness. The little old street lamps, some of which remain, give a faint, glow-worm light in comparison. But ageing folk brood on the past; and I cannot but remember how fine it was, on the winter evenings of the twenties and thirties, to see the lamplighter, Ali Thomson, going on his rounds. He carried a long pole with a little flicker at the end of it. He pushed open a trap at the bottom of the gas lamp with another pole, triggered off the gas inside, up went the igniter; and another corner of Stromness was illuminated. The pole with the flame at the tip of it was a magic wand, driving back the darkness. What a fine, soft, purring light the gas was, too—little globes of radiance here and there about the street, with dark slightly sinister patches in between!... The town council of those days mingled economy with wisdom. On five or six nights round about the full moon there were no street lights at all. The Stromness children of today simply do not know how lovely the town lies under the full moon of winter—it is a magical transfigured place.

Round about midnight the lamplighter went round for the second time and cancelled the lights with his wand. He seemed a hero, in these rain-lashed, windswept tunnels of darkness.

And in the little kitchens of the town in those days, housewives sewed and darned, and schoolchildren did their lessons under the

---

1 Probably Oran, as it turned out later from readers' researches.

dim, soft paraffin lamp set on the dresser. Only in the posher houses was there gaslight. Having implicit faith in the goddess Progress (who is the real deity for most folk nowadays) we waited patiently for electric power: which came in the spring of 1947. And now we have those great glaring eyes all along the street. Our winters are not so beautiful as they used to be.

So powerful has the empire of Progress grown in the past century, that we cannot conceive of the old Orkney crofts with cruisie lamps under the rafters—the feeblest of glims—and old soft mouths at the edge of darkness telling over and over their spells and their stories.

Here Comes Winter

21.10.1971

There other afternoon as I was sitting reading in the rocking chair there was an unusual sound—a rattling, stottering, surging, hissing noise sweeping southwards along the street. I should have known what it was by the preceding gloom and coldness. I looked out of the window and the steps and doorways were fringed with grey sleet. 'So,' I said to myself, 'here comes winter.'

We need not look to have the mild October-to-March that we had last year; when the most that anyone saw in the way of snow was a gentle flurry of flakes lasting half a minute or so. One or other of Mother Carey's chickens shook itself from time to time; there was no wild plucking of the entire flock.

One does not know whether such a smiling winter is acceptable or not. The children have their clogs and sledges all laid out ready in the shed, and nothing happens. The thick polo-necks can't be worn because of the mildness. What about the old folk who have flashes of rheumatism in their shoulders and haunches, and are more liable than anybody to slip on ice, and whose feeble breath is shorn by the frost— surely they welcome a mild winter when it comes? Not a bit of it. They complain more than anybody.

In their opinion a gentle, unseasonable spell doesn't, as winter is meant to do, polish off the germs and all the other invisible beasts and pests that fill our hospitals. 'A green Yule,' they say ominously, 'maks a full kirkyard.'...

But deep under all the proverbs is the powerful instinctive feeling that winter should be winter and summer should be summer, and the loveliness and the flavour of each are squandered by a neutral neither-here-nor-there season. 'There is a time for snow and a time for sun'... 'There is a time for darkness and a time for light'... 'There is a time for the hearth and a time for the wind in the hill'... On such opposites the life of man is woven harmoniously and well.

I read a holiday advertisement in a Sunday paper this week: 'Have summer all the year round'; and it was meant to appeal to monied, modish folk who could, if they so wished, follow the sun to Australia or the Seychelles... After five or six years of that kind of thing a sensitive person, I feel, would be driven half-mad, branded by the intolerable light; and in the end he would spend an entire winter somewhere in the Arctic Circle to heal himself with the beauty of snow and starlight and darkness and cold and the Aurora Borealis.

We ask therefore this winter for one deep, immaculate snowfall, to keep the seeds warm; and for a swift, sudden thaw; and, beyond the mud and wetness, in the new light, the first delicate tremors of spring.

A Web of Byways

28.10.1971

Thousands of tourists come to Stromness every summer and most of them are delighted with our long, surging, twisting street. But I think few of them ever explore the byways—Stromness is such a web of twisting closes that climb halfway up Brinkie's Brae and step down to piers and the sea.

So one Saturday morning recently I took my two friends from 'the sooth' through the town by a wayward, meandering, complex way.

First, we climbed up 'the 44 steps' to the Back Road. It was a calm, mild morning, with rainclouds on the horizon. Then we went down between Dunard and the obliterated site of Queen Street and emerged on to the main street by way of the houses where once Johnny Fiddler and James Miller lived; a fine corner of old Stromness.

Up once more, granitewards and cloudwards—the Bank Lane this time—and behind the new primary school threaded our way; then halfway down the Church Road turned left through the narrow defile beside the Episcopal Church, which opens out on one of the town's loveliest closes, and reached the street again between the sweet factory and the fish and chip shop.

Just across the street is Clouston's pier, always a special place to me because all my earliest memories are of it (the fisherman baiting his lines, the old women swilling headless haddocks, the boys bathing in summer).

There is another enchanting loop going from Church Road to Victoria Street in front of the North Church, all steps and garden. Then we went slowly (it was a warm day and I had taken a duffle for fear of rain) up the Manse Lane, a sequence of brief stone flights, and along Franklin Road, southwards. We would have gone down Khyber Pass, but it was blocked at the bottom where an old house is being restored. Instead we kept to the high road and at Cliff Cottage turned left down another gem of a byway, between gardens, that opens out on to Puffer's Close. Coming down this way you get one of the best views of the town and harbour.

Folk won't be able to stand for very much longer on Gray's Pier, where Stromness's next housing scheme is to be; so we lingered for a while there.

We ended the morning sitting on the seawall at Creig's Pier, and there, if anywhere, you get the taste and flavour of old Stromness— the wash of harbour water and the cry of gulls,

We had timed our eccentric little excursion well. In the afternoon it came on to heavy rain.

Transistors

4.11.1971

I swore I would never buy a transistor radio after having some walks round the west shore flawed by meeting young folk listening mindlessly to the 'pop' brimming out of the black boxes they carried. No not brimming—crashing, screeching, ranting; so that the sounds of nature—the peewits, the rustling cornfield, the waves on the rock—were violated by the insensate noise of men.

But really, one misses so much by not having a radio that can be carried around inside the house. (There is no excuse ever for violating nature's delicate web of sound.) You can listen to a story in the bath. You can carry it downstairs and get some Stravinsky or Bach or Jerome Kern while you are grilling the bacon. You can wake up to the chirpy, satirical comments of Robert Robinson, and be lulled to sleep again by 'A Book at Bedtime'.

But you have to be careful. The riches are endless but you have to ration them anxiously. Too much of music that is generally considered 'good' music can dull the ear, I'm sure. And if you over-indulge in political commentary—on Ulster, the Common Market, atom-bomb testing—the fine edge goes off your own judgment. You can be bludgeoned into hopelessness and apathy.

But on the whole I think a moveable wireless inside a house is a good thing to have. And so when the other week I received a small windfall —a literary prize from France—with part of it I bought a transistor set.

It took a bit of getting to know. It was not just a brutish piece of mechanism. I had to swivel the delicate thing around until it was exactly orientated for the purest reception. It has, too, the invaluable benefit of VHF. Medium wave and long wave have times of crackling and hoarseness. You hoist aloft the slender, stainless steel aerial and depress the VHF knob and you wouldn't believe there could be such clarity.

There are times when you get tired of the inane images of TV. Then what a pleasure it is to indulge that other sensuous organ, the ear...

Councillors

What on earth is the world coming to? Soon, it seems, there will be no Stromness at all; at least, the huddle of houses will always be there between Brinkie's Brae and the sea, but what kind of a town will it be without a provost or bailies or councillors? We can hardly conceive of such a thing. There has always been a provost and a council in Stromness, meeting on the first Monday of every month. Not the oldest inhabitant can recall a time when Stromness was without magistrates (though they tell me we didn't have a provost till some time late in the nineteenth century).

I remember them when I was a small boy—grave men walking with dignity through the street, going and coming from their offices and places of business, lingering to equate their watches with the time on the Old Kirk clock. 'There goes Bailie So-and-So,' the older folk would say; or, 'I wonder what Councillor What's-his-Name is looking at that sewerage pipe for?'... Of course at that tender age we did not know what bailies and councillors were for; but we sensed that they imparted a dignity to the town. They were the topmost stones in the unique pyramid that was Stromness.

That the magistrates had a stern role to play on occasion we learned with awe, when our mothers told us that so-and-so was to appear in the burgh court that day, Bailie Such-and-Such on the bench, for breach of the peace. There were moments of great municipal splendour also. I remember standing in an endless line of school children one day in 1928, waving a little Union Jack, expecting that at any moment Prince George would appear on the crown of Hutchison's Brae, going to name the new lifeboat *'JJKSW'*. There was a great surge of cheers along the street, coming southwards. What unbearable excitement! One hundred tiny flags were shaken. Along the street came a bevy of men, and no one to tell us which of them was the Prince. (I was expecting somebody in glittering armour with a coronet and sword.) But among the troupe was our own Provost Corrigall, and the mere idea that royalty and the chief citizens of Stromness were hobnobbing together that day moved my soul to awe and wonder.

It will never happen any more. I suppose in the end Stromness will not even be a town—it will be 'a municipal unit' or something like that.

First Snow

25.11.1971

It was obvious as soon as you opened your eyes last Wednesday morning that something strange had happened. The bedroom ceiling had an unearthly whiteness. The window was a dead grey rectangle. The snow had come—the first snow of the winter—and it had come early.

When I got out of that cold bed at last and covered my coldness with cold clothes I watched the snow falling on the street and the gardens. It was fine, light incessant stuff, a grey drift. Every smallest twig and wire was loaded. Stromness had vanished overnight, and some Siberian town had been set down in its place. The faces of the folk that passed in the street below looked as though they had been through some very purifying experience.

Snow or sunshine, it's all the same to me, I have to work for my living in a small kitchen with a fan-heater going. (Only this particular morning it had to be boosted to double strength so that I could shave and make the toast without shivering.) For three hours I toiled away with pen and paper and words, and forgot all about the early winterfall. One has at last to come out of one's work trance in order to supply oneself with such necessities as butter and bread and butcher meat—that is to say, shopping must be done in the afternoon.

I opened the door in my duffle coat and sank knee-deep in dazzlement. Stromness was about a foot and a half nearer heaven than it had been on Tuesday. Transfiguration everywhere—but it was my feet that bore the full enchantment. I was wearing a pair of new shoes with smooth leather soles, and that afternoon they dissociated themselves from the rest of my body; they went off on an independent spree. I lurched and slithered everywhere. In Porteous's Brae, because my feet were so wayward, independent and crazy, I almost had a fatal encounter with a huge lorry.

Proceeding northwards along that Stromness street was like stepping from ice floe to ice floe on some Greenland river in spate... Finally, to cure that mad footwork—all these little rushes, glissandos, ballet poses and confrontations with walls—I called on my old friend Mr John Wright the shoemaker, and he provided me with a pair of rubber boots. I walked home then as straight and steady as a guardsman.

As I write this the thaw is under way—perhaps only a temporary thaw, for the sky through the window looks loaded with new snow. And one thinks: November, December, January, February, March— the great whiteness could conceivably span all these months, just to remind us that last year's winter was a kindly aberration.

Ale Brewing

9.12.1971

Nothing is so simple as making a tub of ale. You pour your extract of malt out of the jar into the bin, a long, brown, sticky tongue. Then you dump in a few pounds of sugar, a sudden hailstorm of stickiness. Then you dissolve the lot in hot water. Meantime the brewer is keeping his eye on the hops that are simmering away for the stated hour in the biggest pot in the kitchen. The hops are in a muslin bag; when they boil they give off a smell that is obnoxious to some folk, but I can't say that I mind it. You have nothing to do in the hour of the hop-boiling, so you look fondly at the sticky mixture at the bottom of the bin and perhaps give it an extra stir with the wooden spoon, and you take the scissors to the sachet of yeast, just to be in readiness.

The bag of hops bounces in the broth pot like a plum pudding. You take it out and pour the hop liquor into the stickiness. (Purists of course maintain that there's nothing like the old Orkney brewing kirn, but it really seems to me that a plastic dustbin is as good as anything, and besides, it's much easier to keep clean.)

Everything is now proceeding smoothly to a climax. The next thing you do is fill the bin up to the brim with hot water. Then you simply add the magical ingredient, yeast. This is the key that opens the door, in midwinter, to all the light and gaiety of summers gone. Solemnly sprinkle on to the sticky brown lake the yeast grains. And give the whole thing a sevenfold stir, in sunward circles (it is of course utterly disastrous to do the stirring withershins). And it will do no harm to utter, if you know it, the 'brewer's word'.

Nothing happens, it seems. The yeast pellets have all been stirred into that warm, sweet blackness. They reappear, one by one, like stars on a winter night; then they all appear with one great rush like the stars in Coleridge's poem. The scattered yeast grains coalesce, the mass heaves and multiplies, the whole kirn is possessed by a gentle seething, sighing, whispering. The brew begins to sing.

It is only, then, a question of waiting for the fermentation to be completed, usually in a week or under, then bottling it and waiting for the enchanted liquor to clear in the bottle. And then, some cold, dark, miserable December night, pouring into your pewter mug all the delight of some half-forgotten summer.

Winter Solstice

23.12.1971

When you read this the year will already be on the turn; we will have taken a first hesitant step towards summer; the light will be longer by about half a minute than it was yesterday, the winter solstice.

I wish I could be at Maeshowe at sunset one midwinter day, to see if the light of the setting sun actually does touch, fleetingly, the inner wall of the burial chamber.

These neolithic builders did nothing by accident. You may be sure that there is a meaning in every stone set up, apparently at random, in fields in Stenness and Birsay—symbols of fertility, star measurements, salutes to the sun in its varying stations.

We cannot conceive how eagerly and anxiously those primitive Orkneymen brooded on the scales of summer and winter. After the harvest feast the tribe was fast caught up in the tides of darkness. The grass withered, the animals were butchered, the kindly life-giving sun swung in an ever-narrowing arc through the sky. In December it hardly heaved itself over the Hoy Hills. Its light was weaker—it did not have the great golden power of July.

That ancient Orkney tribe had no reason to believe that the darkness might not go on increasing—the sun might rise no more and all the earth and sea might be bound in an endless frost of death. (Their myths pointed to a perpetual recurrence of light, a renewal out of the death of the year, but there was no guarantee; some year their gods might decree otherwise.) So we must imagine them, as midwinter approached, offering certain fearful sacrifices to the dying sun. The solstice stone in Stenness was red with nourishing blood.

They could not tell whether the 21st or the 22nd was darker. Orkney on both days was a cluster of cold shadows. Was there a faint subtraction of shadows on the 23rd? They could not really be sure— it was a hard thing to tell. (We must credit them with a far higher degree of sensitivity in these matters than ourselves. Their blood registered the subtlest difference of light and darkness.) By noon on the 24th there could be no doubt about it. The light was beginning to return to the world. They were on a tide that would bear them towards the first flowers, the birth of lambs, midsummer, the golden sheaf of corn. At midnight on the 24th of December, at Skara Brae and Brodgar and half a dozen other Orkney villages, there would have been wild rejoicing.

The early Irish monks applied these beliefs to the lives of men. They pointed out, gently, that indeed the promised Light of the World had come at Yule: the merest bud of light, a child in a poor stable in the east.

A Boy at Hogmanay

30.12.1971

In the late evening you would see an anxious knot of men outside Wishart's shop waiting for the last bus out of Kirkwall. They were waiting for their consignments of whisky (for Stromness was as dry as a ten-year-old cork in those days). The men of Stromness bore their precious burdens home from the bus. There are one or two stories of men letting their parcels drop on the cobbles; and standing there, hard strong men whom nothing moved, weeping over broken glass and a splash and a precious rivulet dribbling into the sewer.

It was the only night of the year when boys and girls could stay up till midnight and beyond, and after ten o'clock you began to get slightly tired and bored. It was not like Christmas at all. There were the women cutting up slabs of cake and currant bun. There stood the whisky bottle on the sideboard, surrounded by a gleaming bodyguard of glass. Somewhat apart stood the lesser dignitaries—beer bottles and tumblers.

At ten to midnight your chum called for you and you were thrust into a coat and muffler and you set off, with other groups of dark shadows, towards the Pier Head. There appeared one or two extraordinarily red faces under the lamplight. Suddenly there was a wild hullabulloo from the pier—all the trawlers in the North Sea shrieked their sirens, and at the same time the Pole Star sent up cascades of rockets. Then the people of Stromness came as near to emotion as they ever allowed themselves—there was a fervent shaking of hands, men who maybe hadn't spoken to each other since April met with dewy eyes, they shouted to each other with reckless conviction, 'A Happy New Year!'

For small boys, it was a weird experience.

And once you got home again, about half-past twelve, the night grew stranger. The first-footers began to arrive. You wondered why all those douce men sketched such extravagant gestures in the air, and spoke so loudly, and wanted to kiss every female they saw, and would not be satisfied until they were launched into a sea of songs. Occasionally you saw a white, sick mask of a face, or eyes with an angry glower in them. Between the songs there was an incessant tinkle of glass. The paraffin lamp on the dresser threw a rich, muted light over everything.

It was on one of those New Year's mornings that I had a shattering experience. (Being young, you felt rather out of things—Christmas was your time.) I wondered why the yellow liquid in the small glasses should alter the characters of everybody to such an extent—make them all into clowns or heroes. So when my father was up singing an Edwardian ballad, I touched his glass to my lips. Never, never had I tasted anything so hideous! It took tears of revulsion to my eyes. I vowed silently that the stuff would never pass my lips again—no, indeed, I was perfectly happy as I was...

After a few years, however, I acquired a certain liking for the stuff.

January

6.1.1972

January is the month when for a morning or two you expect to wake up with a dry mouth at least.

January is the month when you observe, sadly, six of your seven good resolutions blow away on the cold wind.

January is the month when you dismantle—on a precise date, the sixth—the Christmas tree and give all those expensive Christmas cards to the children to scrawl on with their crayons.

January is the month when bills seem to seep through your letter box with pitiless monotony. The man who was as rich as Rockefeller on Christmas Eve is as poor now as a church mouse.

January is the month when you wait for the worst of the winter to fall, sleet and hail and snow out of the north-east. You kind of exist between an iron earth and a leaden sky.

January is the month when turkey and sauterne and tangerines are forgotten about for another eleven months. You are grateful for simple things—a fire, a bowl of soup, a piece of bread.

January is the month of Robbie Burns, that marvellous man whose memory has been ruined in great splurges of sentimentality and hogwash.

January is the month when you go through a box of tissue handkerchiefs a week.

January is the month of the double mask. It looks both ways, into the follies and delights of the past year, and into the nebulous hopes of what is to come. Either way, it tells you very little.

January is the month when you are appalled by the number of empty screwtops in your cupboard. Hopefully you order more malt, more sugar, more hops.

January used to be the month when the people of Orkney read books. Now we grow sick on a surfeit of television. Imagination in the north, which used to be most vivid at this time of year, slowly withers.

January is the month of rubber boots and bonnets and the mittens Aunty Bella knitted.

January is the month when bed is the most beautiful place of all. The eight o'clock news on the bedside wireless is a hateful sound. You rise and have to lay aside all those beautiful swathings of dream.

January is the month when the full moon is most glorious of all (though I think the stars have it, for December).

There is no month of the year quite like January. What is better than a walk along the west shore in that cold, silver air?

Burns' Night

20.1.1972

Next week Orkney will once more be celebrating Robbie Burns. (Pity the poor Shetlanders, who also have Up-Helly Aa that same night!) Most of us will be giving a passing thought, at least, to a figure we all cherish in our imaginations. There he stands, his head tilted meditatively on his fingers, looking at a mountain daisy or a mouse. Poetical thoughts go through his mind.

But then he takes a tumble to himself—this won't do, he has to plough the whole rig before it gets dark. The darkness!—other thoughts come to him as he whips up the horses. There will be a glass of whisky and a mug of 'tipenny ale' in 'Poosie Nansie's'. There will be bawdy jokes round the fire, each one followed by a great gale of laughter. The ploughman from Mossgiel Farm with the black eyes and thick shoulders is the most extravagant raconteur of all; and with him too the general crudity of the stories has a verve and style and polish.

But he cannot drink too much *uisge beatha*, for his stomach is more delicate than most drinkers. He leaves early. He must be up and in the stable again before the sun gets up. He walks along the hillside resolutely. He has made up his mind to attend to his farm from now on. There has been too much frivolity in his life—it won't do—there is the rent to be paid and his father sick and he is the eldest of the family, the breadwinner. One thing he will not give up, however; the few books he has in the attic—Addison, Fergusson, Pope. If it wasn't for his books and his pen and paper, life would not be worth living. But life is there to be lived, and it is a stern, hard, austere business, and there is a deity to answer to when it is all over.

The two-horned moon has risen over the Cumnock hills...

What is that among the trees? He hears a small trill of laughter, the swish of a skirt. He is being observed. The ploughman stands stock still on the road. He had not bargained for this. He knows that sweet-mouthed ghost among the trunks—he has exchanged a word with her at the Tarbolton Fair only on Tuesday: a few jesting phrases, a flash of laughter, a black smoulder of the eyes... He does not even know her name yet, but it is obvious she has made enquiries as to the road that the merry-mouthed ploughman takes home at nights, after his dram or two.

As he stands there, rooted, a great sweet, ungovernable surge of desire rises through him. He is aware of nothing else—duty, religion, freemasonry, farming—because of the powerful, fecund thundering of his heart. Again he hears it, the shy mockery from the wood...

But all these bits of biography are, in a sense, irrelevant—dangerous, indeed, for we tend to sentimentalise everything connected with this man. The only important thing is that, by some divine accident, Robert Burns happened to be a great, marvellous, thrilling poet, the best that Scotland has produced since the old anonymous ballad-men.

Influenza

27.1.1972

It's a bit dangerous, living in Orkney these days—almost as bad as being a Londoner in 1665. It is this flu that is scything down our noblest and best. There they lie, shivering in bed, with aspirins, antibiotics, hot lemon drinks and transistors on the bedside table, smiling wanly at any visitor who is bold enough to enter the chamber of suffering.

All one week the Stromnessians were going down like ninepins. The lucky ones thought between apprehension and joy, 'I've come through so far—I might get away with it'—rather like a soldier at the Somme running on while the front line crumples around him.

As day follows day, confidence mounts. I exulted in the great wind of Sunday evening that blew acres of torn spindrift across the street, through every seaward opening. On Monday morning when I did my shopping the gale was worse still. Between Mayburn Court and Graham Place the street was empty. It was a rather uncanny feeling; the wind howling dementedly up every close, and not one face at a door or a window... 'What if every single soul in Stromness has been smitten with flu but you alone,' I said to myself. It was a moment dangerously close to hubris, the overweening pride that—the Greeks considered—always comes before a 'humpty-dumpty'.

But after Graham Place a few townsfolk manifested themselves, frail shoppers in the storm.

The day following—Tuesday—was a day that can only be described as hideous. It was a day when the heartiest souls that ever lived— Billy Bunter, Micawber, Falstaff—would have been in the dumps. I have never heard such a snarl on the lips of the wind. I would not dream of complaining about the fine little house I rent from the council; but all of Tuesday it shuddered; it strained on its foundations; it was full of a hundred little icy draughts that stabbed like conspirators. But, anyhow, I sat at my table and worked away at the day's diary; for, thought I complacently, the elements can't do a thing to me, not this winter...

What was that in my right nostril in mid-afternoon? It seemed to be stuffed with pepper. And what had become of all the weekend exhilaration? The world was suddenly a grey, uninteresting place—'a sterile promontory', as Hamlet put it—it seemed to me that nothing really gay or exciting was ever likely to happen again on this planet. Also I didn't like the way my bronchial tubes were rasping, as if a dozen small men with files were down there, deep inside my chest, scraping and scratching away. My leaden reverie was shattered by the bursting of the peppercorn in my nose. I had sneezed like a man possessed...

In due course—need I tell the rest of the story?—there I was, propped up on pillows, with Lucozade beside me, and bottles of pills, and a few magazines, like hundreds of other Stromnessians. The only difference was that I didn't have a grand thing like flu at all—it was only a bit of a cold.

North End v South End

10.2.1972

One of the tensions that made life in Stromness interesting forty years ago was the rivalry between the North End and the South End. The hostility was confined entirely to the boys of the town—girls and adults could pass freely across the frontier... Where was the frontier? That was the first point in dispute. The Northenders claimed that it was the burn that came from the hills and flowed under Graham Place. The Southenders said that it was the Kirk Road. Looking back at the question now, it seems that the North End was probably right. But it was important, because some of the best of the young footballers stayed in the disputed territory.

The North-South rivalry found its most agreeable expression in football matches. There were occasional unfortunate encounters. Nobody in those days could afford 'colours'; we played in our ordinary clothes, a wild mêlée of purple, white, red, grey, black. We could not afford goalposts either—we had to make do with heaps of coats, or stones. There were endless disputes as to whether the ball had gone 'in' or 'out', or was 'too high'—the invisible crossbar was adjudged to be the height of the goalkeeper's upstretched arm, a very imprecise measure. In fact a goal was nearly always disputed, in the absence of a net which makes every goal palpable.

I remember one hot day in the summer holidays when a group of Northenders and Southenders were wandering along the road to the west shore (it must have been to bathe). Football was out of the question in that oven of a day. But the needle was still there, between 'the boys of summer'.

'The South End,' said a Southender idly, 'has got the shore.'

'That's nothing,' said a Northender. 'The North End has the Pier.'

'The Museum,' said another, 'is in the South End.'

'The School,' said another, 'is in the North End.' (But that was a doubtful asset to claim.)

'We have the Library'...

'We have the Auction Mart'...

'We have the Town Hall'...

'We have the Market Green'...

'The Lifeboat'...

'The Police Station'...

'The Pole Star'...

So the group of boys walked towards the sea, dredging institutions of importance and splendour out of their section of the town—Login's Well, Stromness Hotel, War Memorial... (The Kirks must have been a bit of a problem, since all three of them lay in disputed territory.)

The boys stood on the sea-banks for a long time, stinging each other like bees.

Nowadays that old rivalry seems to have completely withered away among the young—and whether that is a good or a bad thing I would not care to say.

Journey to Perth

2.3.1972

On the way to Perth there was one golden afternoon in Aberdeen (it was a leisurely journey, as you can see). In the Aberdeen Art Gallery you can get a good cup of coffee and sit for as long as you like writing postcards to your friends back home. It was still a bit cold outside, but the sun had a new vernal burnish and there were only a few high, white clouds. After living for a long while in a community where everyone is known to everyone else there is something pleasurable and exhilarating in walking unknown among crowds of strangers. There is a handsome pub in Union Street, a rare piece of Victoriana, where only men can drink. It was pleasant too to sit there for an hour over a pint of Guinness and ham sandwiches, and hear all around the hewn granite speech of the north-east.

I had never taken a train to Perth before, and somehow I imagined we would cross the Grampians. But we didn't; we went the old familiar route through Stonehaven, Montrose, Arbroath; and at Dundee veered inland to the heart of Scotland. (I will speak about coffee again, at the risk of boring everyone. A cup of coffee on the train cost eleven new pence. I made a rapid calculation—in the old money it comes to approximately two shillings and twopence-halfpenny...) At Dundee I saw another Orkneyman, Eric Linklater, getting off the train.

Perth manifested itself first in a gleam of inland water with swans on it, the Tay. There is a smart new railway station. (In the buffet there, for some reason, the coffee cost only seven new pence a cup, and it was just as good as the elevenpence brew, and the same lot, British Railways, sold it.)

I had never been to Perth before, other than passing through it in a bus at night, in the old days when the only transport I could afford between Edinburgh and Scrabster was the overnight summer season bus. At Perth in those days there was a transport cafe where bus-travellers got rolls and tea before plunging, in deepening cold and darkness, through the Highlands... The other day I took a taxi to Perth Theatre, and deposited my meagre luggage there, and was shown along a dim corridor where something was happening on the candle-splashed stage. It was another Orkneyman, David Birch, taking the players through part of a rehearsal of my play *A Spell for Green Corn* (that was the reason why I was there). The theatre that day was a huge cave of gloom because I had arrived in time to experience a thing that Orcadians had got off with, a power cut. The players looked at their scripts by the light of pocket torches. In spite of all that, everyone seemed carefree and gay. Presently someone gave me a cup of coffee for nothing.

Perth Theatre

9.3.1972

Perth Theatre, right in the heart of the city, is a delightful place. The main door opening on to the High Street is available all day. Anybody can walk in from the street and mount the stairs and sit down in the foyer for a pleasant half-hour over coffee and biscuits. All around the business of the theatre is going on—tickets being sold, bookings taken at the box office, and the actors and technicians mingling intimately with the public... Inside, the auditorium is small but finely proportioned, with a steep gallery, and even boxes where you would be more conspicuous than the players on the stage, but from where (it seems to me) you would only see a segment of the stage.

I went the other night to see the opening of J. M. Barrie's early twentieth-century comedy, *The Admirable Crichton*. A vaguely socialistic English peer, Lord Brocklehurst, is about to take his family on a tropical cruise on his yacht. At the last minute he takes his butler, Crichton, a man who frigidly disapproves of his master's ideas (though loyal to the point of obsequiousness). The yacht is wrecked on a desert island. There all the rigid distinctions of England are violently shaken up. Nature sorts everyone out. The new master of the situation is Crichton, who knows how to light a fire and sink a well and knock down trees. He is the King of the Island...

In the end, of course, they are rescued by the beacon that Crichton has constructed to summon a passing ship, and back in England the old pattern re-establishes itself.

It was beautifully performed and enthusiastically received.

Meantime the theatre folk are busily rehearsing the play in which I am concerned, and several of the actors in *The Admirable Crichton* are in that too, so that they have two instruments to perform on at the same time. What is admirable, in an outside world of nagging and grousing, is how gay and dedicated these young players are. They bring enthusiasm and the greatest care to their performances. They love their work, and it shows in their attitude to each other and to the world.

Perth itself is a busy prosperous town. The sense of history broods everywhere. Scone where the old Scottish Kings were crowned is only two miles away. The hotel where I am staying once housed for a night or two Charles Edward Stuart on his way to Edinburgh, Derby, and Culloden.

I walked to the end of a street one day and came suddenly on the Tay, a wide tranquil river that draws its waters from the central Highlands and pours them into the North Sea. And there are tree-clad mountains all around that, I am told, offer magnificent views. Some day soon, perhaps, someone will take me to the foothills in a car.

Spring in the Highlands

16.3.1972

Spring is spreading swiftly over Scotland. There are crocuses in the grass, the branches are tightly studded with buds, the sky when it opens is a deeper, warmer blue. Yet nearly everyone in the company I've been keeping lately is sniffing, coughing, sneezing. I've been told more than once that Perth, lying between the mountains and the river, is not a good place for respiratory ailments. I suppose every beautiful place has a drawback of some kind.

One Saturday morning I took a bus to the royal burgh of Falkland in the interior of Fife, to visit my friends, Kulgin Duval and Colin Hamilton. The journey started in a splash of sunlight. Halfway there a massive black cloud crashed soundlessly into a hillside, and the bus moved on in deluges of hail. Winter never leaves us without a few reminders of his reign. Next morning the beautifully shaped hill outside my window, usually a brown and green dapple at this time of year, stood all white in the Sabbath sun.

The Royal Stuarts built a palace in Falkland, and it is still there, a great attraction to tourists in the summer. In the chapel of the palace, where James the Fifth and Mary Queen of Scots worshipped, Mass is still said for the Catholics of the area. The ancient walls are lined with enormous tapestries. The sanctuary light burns across the centuries. An English priest said the Mass for the Third Sunday in Lent.

My friends, after seven years of residence, are leaving Falkland for a new house on the shore of Loch Tummel, fifty miles away. This was their last Sunday in that medieval Fife town. In the afternoon we went by car to see what progress the workmen were making with the new house. Out of Perth the road wound upwards into the heart of the Highlands. Yesterday's snow had left white scars on the flanks of the mountains. The distant hills were high white gleams.

The wild lonely places are becoming ever more precious and rare in a world dedicated to speed and power and sordidness. Here and there, among immense spaces of 'wildness and wet', was a farm or a shepherd's bothy or a little school. The narrow road seemed to career full tilt at the base of a mountain-mass that filled the entire windscreen; then swerved aside at the last minute; and new mountains gathered silently and awesomely around.

The car ran along the shore of a lovely narrow loch, and stopped in a half-flagged courtyard. My friends had taken over an old farm; they have demolished the dwelling-house and restored the steading. After two years what they have now, in that lonely place between the mountains and the loch, is one of the most handsome, comfortable homes I have ever seen.

There was still, that Sunday, plenty of work to be done in and around the house; but they were going to move in permanently four days later.

'The Dearest Freshness'

23.3.1972

The worst pollution that used to afflict Orkney were the strewments of farmhouse rubbish on the shore here and there. The farmers, having no 'ashie-kert' to uplift their rubbish, dumped it 'afore the face' from time to time. The townsfolk grumbled. Those sauce bottles and empty syrup tins spoiled their Sunday afternoon walks. In fact that kind of dumping, though unsightly for a week or two, is innocent enough. Nature quickly absorbs it. The tins rust away, the broken bottles, which might be dangerous to bathers, are worn away at last to smooth, flat, opaque pebbles.

The years have brought more sinister kinds of pollution—the smirr of oil that ruins a child's afternoon at the beach. It has drifted from a ship in mid-Atlantic—there is simply nothing that anyone can do about it. The increasing use of plastic containers has complicated the situation too. One looker into the future has had an appalling vision of civilisation being smothered under a mountain of indestructible plastic.

There is a kind of beauty in broken glass and rusting tin—a foreshore strewn with plastic remnants looks sinister, as though they were the leavings of the Daleks.

But in the end even plastic bottles and oil slicks may seem innocent enough compared to the frightful kinds of pollution that the future holds. Indeed they may be already upon us; radioactive effluents of lead and mercury and uranium. No men in history have been so arrogant as the scientists in their rummaging and ransacking of nature. The generations to come may have to pay dearly for the little triumphs they have won for humanity—the gramophone, the internal combustion engine, the television screen, DDT, atomic energy.

We must have faith that somewhere, deep down at the very roots and sources of life, there is an endless upsurge of health and renewal. (If there were not, the earth would have shrivelled like a rotten apple millenniums since.) A hundred years ago the poet Gerard Manley Hopkins, troubled by the pollution of industrial England, consoled himself with the certainty that 'there lives the dearest freshness deep down things' ...

We can only hope that that primal unsullied source will be strong enough to wash away the frightful poisons that men are pouring into the air and earth and oceans every hour of the day and night.

So, nowadays, when I take an afternoon walk around the coast, I am not offended any more by the empty sauce bottles and syrup tins on the rocks below. They seem to be simple human friendly objects. The freshness of nature, that lives 'deep down things', passes over them, and they are gone.

Gray's Pier

6.4.1972

After the dance of the bulldozers, Gray's Pier is no more. When I got back from Perth at the end of March, there was a tall wooden stockade along the seaward side of the street, and a padlocked gate. One could glimpse, in working hours, the death-throes of the pier— great holes had been trenched in it; the kindly surface had been churned to a quagmire.

Gray's Inn, which stood between the pier and Dundas Street, was knocked down a couple of years ago. Those present at its demise might have seen the deep well whence Mr Gray—whatever eighteenth-century Stromness taverner he was—drew the water to make his ale and, possibly, whisky. A month ago the Britannia Inn next door was levelled with the earth. It must have been a famous drinking street at one time, rather like Rose Street in Edinburgh...

Gray's Pier was where all the boys in that part of the town used to play in the thirties. There we lowered our limpet-baited sillock lines, and waited patiently, sometimes all morning, for a single silver sklinter to flash in the sunlight, momentarily, before it was given to some mewing cat.

Sometimes a crab came up—such a useless stupid little brown hunchback—and was laid on the flagstone at the edge of the pier. If it was lucky it smelt the sea and made a diagonal scuttle back over the edge. It sometimes happened, alas, that a boy with hobnailed boots would jump close-footed on it; there was nothing of that crab then but fragments of shell on the pier and a vivid yellow splash.

From the small boats at the slip, with the fishermen's permission, we would push off and row towards the '*Ola*'s waves', when the old ship spread her furrows shorewards in the late afternoon.

At the top of the close lived Coxswain Johnston and his wife, as sweet an old couple as you could wish for—he was the hero of the *Carmenia II* rescue at the Kirk Rocks in 1928.

The Lifeboat Shed itself was close by. Gray's Pier was normally occupied by a few fishermen, cats, boys with wands, on a summer day. But let the twin rockets explode in the clouds above Stromness, and then Gray's

Pier was as thronged as ever it was in the herring-fishing days; half the folk of Stromness wondering, speculating, watching... Presently the old *JJKSW*[1] hurtled down the slip and met the sea in a superb cleaving of the waters; then settled, steadied, and made for the west...

That piece of drama will have to be viewed, in future, from some other grandstand.

Oil, Gold, Uranium

13.4.1972

We had better relish the flavour of every day we live from now on, because very soon the life of the place is going to be radically altered. Oil is going to change everything. There was a map of Scotland in *The Scotsman* a week or two back that showed the areas of undersea oil. There were two patches on either side of Orkney.

It seems possible therefore that there may be oil somewhere under Wideford Hill or the Loons. Indeed, some Orkney folk have been declaring for decades that Orkney is floating on oil. 'Look at those marshy bits in the Loons,' they say. 'You can see the skim of oil on the surface of the water...'

And so you can, but hitherto it has been generally accepted as some kind of vegetation excretion. Soon there may be great spouting geysers at the back of Brinkie's Brae.

But there is more than oil in Orkney; somebody has discovered traces of uranium at Yesnaby. There was a Stromness man in my childhood who had a matchbox full of tiny nuggets of gold, about the size of pinheads, that he had found in the burn at Mooseland, he said.

So, between oil wells, gold mines and uranium mines, we can bid a swift farewell to the Orkney we know—the Orkney of Robert Rendall's lyrics and of the agricultural cycle as described in *Reminiscences of an Orkney Parish*. That Orkney is about to vanish as drastically as Pictish Orkney once the Vikings arrived.

---

1 The Stromness lifeboat for a quarter of a century.

Much that is wonderful and precious and irreplaceable will be no more.

Yet there is a certain amount of hypocrisy in those nostalgic backward glances. 'Suppose,' I keep telling myself, 'you were to be walking out beyond Warbeth, and you kicked a pebble—and, impressed by its hardness and heaviness, picked it up and found that you had an uncut diamond in your hand—and later found two or three more diamonds in the same place—what then? There would be less talk of the wistful past of Orkney; your mind would be one wild delirium concerning your own private jewel-strewn future.'

The Sabbath Breaker

27.4.1972

Last week[1] we followed the Rev Peter Learmonth through Stromness, to find out the number of ale houses along the street in the year 1839. He was somewhat shocked and shaken to discover that there were 38.

This week, we will take a sideways glance at another ecclesiastic figure from the early nineteenth century. There he stands, John Louttit, Kirk Officer of the Secession Church, appointed 22nd March 1814, with a harpoon in one hand and the big Kirk bible under his other arm.

The Kirk Session had given long and anxious consideration to the appointment of its first Kirk officer. They debated the matter for six months and more. He must above all be a pious and good-living man. The election fell upon John Louttit. His salary was to be one guinea a year, plus threepence at every baptism.

For more than eight years we must assume that John Louttit performed his office faithfully and well: carrying up the bible to the pulpit on the Sabbath, keeping the new building above the Plainstones swept and garnished, touching his forelock to the elders in the kirk door.

Then, suddenly, a dreadful thing happened. On 15th October 1822, John Louttit was charged with Sabbath profanation. It was as if a thunderbolt had fallen into the sheepfold.

---

1 That article is not included in this selection.

What had happened, it seems, was that early one Sunday morning John Louttit was lighting his blink of fire in his house at the pier (and it was a terrible job sometimes to get those red peats from the side of Brinkie's Brae to take light) when he heard folk running along the street, and the sound of boats being pushed down the nousts. 'Tut-tut,' said John Louttit. He made his breakfast, a poor meal of bread and buttermilk. (You could hardly live like a king on a guinea a year.)

More young men ran past his window. Oars splashed in the harbour. The women—who should have been putting on their best grey shawls for the morning service—were clucking like hens in every door. John Louttit heard the word 'whales'. That was the cause of all the excitement. There was a school of whales somewhere in the west. The pagans of Stromness were setting forth—Sabbath or no—for the great round-up and slaughter.

John Louttit, putting on his stiff white collar, debated the matter seriously. He was one of the best whale hunters in Orkney. Nothing delighted him more than to yell and clash metal behind a blundering panic-stricken herd; until at last, in blind panic, they hurled themselves to death on the beach at Warbeth or Billia-Croo. Then it was time for the knives and the barrels. John Louttit saw in his mind's eye, with great vividness, the red whale steaks. Well salted, a man could live off them all winter. He could sit up late, over a yarn and a dram, by the light of a tallow candle that came out of the whale also.

Sabbath profanation was a serious matter. On the other hand, a man was permitted on such a day to do 'works of necessity and mercy'. Winter was coming on and John Louttit's cupboard was not over-stocked. A guinea a year was not a princely salary... John Louttit removed his stiff, high, white collar. He took the sharp flensing knife from the cupboard. He put on his oldest moleskin trousers; they were likely to be well spattered with blood before sundown. John Louttit took down the oars from the rafters. He went gravely down the steps to his dinghy.

The minister had to carry the bible up to the pulpit himself that Sabbath. A week after the original charge, John Louttit made a second appearance before the Session. It is recorded that, at the meeting of 22nd October, 'he did not express that sense of the evil of such a notorious profanation of the Lord's day as was wished or expected. It was agreed that he should be rebuked before the congregation on Saturday first.'

That is the one brief tantalising glimpse that we have of John Louttit. There is no end to the story. We have no idea whether he was sacked in disgrace, or reinstated; if so, perhaps he had to give all his whale meat and tallow to the poor, and go on living piously and poorly on his salary of fourpence a week.

Daffodils

4.5.1972

I took the bus to Kirkwall the other Thursday afternoon. It was a cold day, dappled with sun and cloud. There is some special pleasure in travelling by bus which the hectic car-drivers miss; perhaps because the journey is more leisurely, with pleasant stops here and there for the delivery of a parcel; and also because you sit at a higher elevation, and can see all that much more of the landscape. Cars nowadays are too smooth and well-sprung; travelling by bus you get the occasional rattle and jolt that recalls no doubt ancestral memories of stage coaches.

I think it was the daffodils that gave a special delight to the Stromness-Kirkwall road that day. I have been told that the WRI ladies have encouraged the growing of daffodils beside the roads. If so, all credit to them. At Tormiston and Finstown there were great golden drifts of them; here and there smaller but no less lovely patches; an occasional lonely trumpet of light at a croft wall. There is something special about the daffodils. There may be other lovelier flowers—roses and tulips—but the daffodil is specially dear because it is a part of the great wave of light that surges over the world in March. It is the colour of the sun, and yet there is a coldness and purity in the blossom as if it remembered the snow.

The poets have always had a special regard for the daffodil. Shakespeare in his catalogue of the flowers speaks of:

'...daffodils,
That come before the swallow dares, and take
The winds of March with beauty...'

The learning of poetry by rote in school has put many people off Wordsworth, to their great loss. But his lyric about the daffodils survives the blind millstones:

'...all at once I saw a crowd,
A host, of golden daffodils;
Beside the lake, beneath the trees,
Fluttering and dancing in the breeze...'

Perhaps there is a sadness in the flower, expressed by another seventeenth-century poet:

'Fair daffodils, we weep to see
You haste away so soon...'

They are so fleeting; they remind us of mortality. The daffodils will not be here when 'the high midsummer pomps come on...'

But another mouth, in Galilee two thousand years ago, touched the daffodil—tissue of sun and wind and snow—to divine immortality:

'Consider the lilies of the field, how they grow. They toil not, neither do they spin. But yet I say unto you, that Solomon in all his glory was not arrayed as one of these...'

That loveliness has come and gone on the spring wind for all those thousands of years. Even in the depths of winter their inevitable oncoming should give us a lift of the heart.

Advice to Tourists

18.5.1972

Well, stranger, if you really want to come to Stromness for the first time some time this summer, I think you should come in June, before the torrent of tourists starts. I don't think I would come in Shopping Week, for example, for then you don't see a typical Stromness at all; the loudspeakers and flags and 'groups' and yards-of-ale are brought out especially for the occasion.

But June is a time of marvellous light and freshness, and it is still quiet.

Once you step off the *St Ola*, your feet will soon find a way to the best places. But mention ought to be made of a special few places, for it is easy to miss them. For example, nearly every visitor is enchanted with our one long, plunging, winding street—so much so that he omits to wander off up one of the closes—Manse Lane or Khyber Pass—or down one of the small piers with its boats and creels. Stromness is a fascinating web of stone.

And when you wander up one of these closes your feet should never stop until they arrive at the summit of Brinkie's Brae. (Don't ask me who Brinkie was—it is one of the mysteries—nobody in Stromness can tell you—in the old maps it is simply called the Ward Hill.) From Brinkie's the view is marvellous—a gleam of lochs, hovering hawks, Hoy and the Atlantic, Scapa Flow, the huddle of grey houses at your feet.

Or follow the road westward past the Golf Course, allowing your eyes not to be hurt too much by the military debris, and you will come to a kirkyard beside the sea with the remnants of a chapel and (perhaps) a monastery wall. Here the family history of Stromness is told on heavy stone pages. Beyond is the lovely beach of Warbeth; and the crumbling Hall of Breckness; and a cliff to put awe on you, the Black Craig.

In the opposite direction the limit of Stromness is the Brig-o-Waithe. A very talented Orkney poet called it 'no a bonny place, neither here nor there'... But here history was made one terrible Saturday night in March 1940 when a German pilot scattered his bombs about the hamlet and killed the first British civilian of the war. The poet— Anne Scott-Moncrieff—was writing about that very event. She went on to speak about 'Waithe, that wreaths the salt tides wi' the fresh'... Below the bridge the waters meet; the bitterness of the sea is mingled with the sweet inland waters. There is beauty in the place after all, in spite of the ordinary fields surrounding it; and well the poet knew it.

A Literary Gathering

1.6.1972

How frustrating it is, when you are hoping to be home tomorrow, to catch up with the load of work you have left undone, to be told by BEA that there are no seats available, nor for the three following days. It looks as if the summer rush to the north has started early this year.

However, there are compensations. I might be stuck for days in some bed-and-breakfast garret, but here I am in a kind house full of books and good food and conversation.

It is only four days since I left Orkney. In Edinburgh there was a literary gathering, a cocktail party for my new book *Greenvoe*. In elegant eighteenth-century rooms in the Lawnmarket were gathered booksellers, librarians, publishers, authors, critics, journalists. Whisky, champagne and gin circulated in one direction, and smoked salmon, cheese, etc in another. And for two hours and more the literary folk mingled and met and drifted apart, in an air of increasing euphoria and bonhomie (well, in most instances).

But, though it is exhilarating at the time, it is a strain having to speak to so many folk, and next morning I was pretty tired. It is pleasant coming to consciousness in the city of Edinburgh at this time of year, with tall trees all round the house shimmering with new tender foliage, and the blossoms tossed by the wind like a pink snowstorm, and the sky above the Castle all a surge of blue sky and cloud.

Soon, after a beer and a sausage roll, it was time to get back to Aberdeen. Beyond the new Forth Road Bridge, which is a marvellous structure from every point of view, the brain begins to grow numb with the endless ribbon of road. What strikes the traveller new from Orkney, perhaps, is the power and size of the new lorries. One thinks, probably ignorantly, that the railways would be far better handling such freight than the roads, which are dangerous enough without these trundling monsters.

After three hours the spires of Aberdeen pierced the northern sky. At home we ate a marvellous meal of soup and flounders. In the sitting room of this most hospitable house are swivelling black-leather easy chairs where you can either sit upright or lie, supine and horizontal, in splendid luxury.

I thought, nodding on this splendid contrivance on the verge of sleep, that soon this brief interlude will be over; but just now the voice from the BEA office has given me a douche of cold water. However—as I said—what better place to be stranded?

'The Orkney Croft'

8.6.1972

'The Orkney Croft' is the title of this summer's exhibition in Stromness Museum. It looks at life in Orkney, mainly agricultural life, nearly a century ago, before the great machines drove off the horses and broke to a large extent the ancient rhythms. Much use is made of contemporary implements, which were tools and symbols at the same time, but the exhibition rests principally on the skilful deployment of a superb set of old photographs. The photos have been 'blown up', and the enlargement actually gives them more life. authenticity, and atmosphere. (Looking at postcard size photographs is like seeing life through the wrong end of a telescope: all is neat, Lilliputian, somehow unreal.)

The life of our ancestors is all here. The horse and ox are ploughing together. An old reaper is 'sharping' his scythe on a stone. Peat-cutters are having their dinner on the hill. Terrified cattle are winched into holds. People search for food in rockpools or along the face of crags. Here are the days of rejoicing, when the man from Orphir and the man from Birsay come together for the only occasion in the year—the Dounby Show. There are the sail-yawls and the spinning wheels and the looms. You can see the legendary characters out of last century—Skatehorn, Annie Harper.

It is a memorable exhibition, one of the best that the Museum has put on (and that's saying something). I have been to see it twice and I hope to go back a few times yet before September. The quiet faces that look back at us are near enough in time—they are our grandparents and great-grandparents—and yet they contemplate us across an enormous chasm. Time has accelerated since their day, and is still accelerating, and has taken us far from their region of poverty and simplicity.

The exhibition has been planned and set up by Bryce Wilson. He ought to be congratulated on a beautiful and masterly evocation.

An Atlantic-fronting Seapink

22.6.1972

Here we are, near midsummer, and how pleasant it would be, among all these dull days, to have a splash or two of sunshine. The weather has been meagre with his gold as a miser this year.

Sun or no, one has to get some fresh air after a long morning at pen and paper. So I set off last Thursday afternoon—Stromness being all locked up with the 'half holiday'—to walk to the west. It was a strange hushed dull kind of day—it couldn't make up its mind to rain or shine, or remain just neutral.

For sometimes the high grey fleece of cloud would shred out and grow threadbare, and a few blue holes were torn in the sky. And you would think, 'Good, the sun's going to shine...' But the next minute the blue rents were quickly drawn together and stitched up; and the gleam vanished from Stromness harbour.

In the folds of Hoy there was a veil of rain. Graemsay dulled. Then you would think, regretting not having taken a pacamac, 'It's going to rain...' Sure enough, a thin smirr dampened the face and put spots on the stones of the road. But you could scarcely call it rain—it was just a damp breath, a ghostly precipitation—and it was over in half a minute. And there once more over Breckness blue holes were being torn in the sky, and a fleeting brightness went over Outertown.

There is a long sloping wedge of rock that runs from the Nethertown road out into Hoy Sound. (I think it is called Ramna, but I will have to look up the 25-inch map.) The high tide covers most of it, but at low tide you can venture down to the seaweed and the pools and feel that you are on the prow of a ship, with the advancing waters crashing and surging on both sides of you. The sloping, tilted surface is broken into neat squares, as though nature had some plan in mind. And as though nature had some lesson in bravery and joy for us, there, rooted between two of these squares, a seapink was growing—in the very teeth of the sea, the foremost of a host of seapinks that grew in comparative safety higher up among 'cocks-and-hens', buttercups, daisies.

At home, I turned on the telly. Strikes, murders, Ireland, air crashes, inflation. Through the window the day had settled into a steady greyness. That solitary Atlantic-defying seapink was the most hopeful thing the day had brought forth. I felt, perhaps foolishly, that it was a symbol of something.

Midsummer

6.7.1972

It is Midsummer Day as I write—as always a magical time of the year, when our hemisphere leans closest to the sun—and yet the people are going about their business as though nothing had happened. There was one marvellous day early in the week when the hills and sea lay soaked in light.

The truth is, I suppose, that we are not so dependent on the sun nowadays. He has not stored the hills with peat. He will not bring the corn to its final harvest burnish and so ensure food and ale for the winter to come. The sun has lost much of his power and glory. For us readers of encyclopaedias there is a blind blundering ball of fire ninety million miles away. We like it when the sun shines—then, we can have a picnic on the beach, and drink iced lager. Increasing numbers of us can go in search of the sun to Majorca or Greece. How pleasant to have a deep tan for a month or two.

Our ignorant great-grandfathers had a relationship with the sun that was intense and meaningful. Midsummer for them was a mysterious time. For days before Johnsmas the crofters and their wives and bairns carried fuel to the summit of the highest hill in the district. They must have performed the ritual solemnly, as if their lives and livelihoods depended on it. Ever since Yule the sun had been climbing the sky with increasing power and majesty. Because of the sun their beasts had multiplied and their corn was green. They must show their gratitude to the sun with their small mortal fires.

Reverently, near midnight on 23rd June, a torch was thrust into the pyre—the flames crepitated and clustered—at last the hilltop was one crimson fire. Then all awe and fearfulness were sunk in night-long joy. There was dancing, there was leaping through the flames. Before dawn every crofter lit a small private torch at the fire and carried it round his own fields and house and steading. So his land was purified with the sacred fire. He had kept his pledge to the life-giving sun.

Nowadays we just get tanned, and drink iced lager, and have a little holiday.

The Young Invaders

13.7.1972

Stromness is being pleasantly invaded by troops of young folk. Some of them stay in tents at Ness, but most of them are billeted in the Town Hall in Hellihole (now the Youth Hostel). Ever since the end of the war young people have been coming to Orkney, but never in such numbers as in recent years. The summer of 1972 promises to break all records.

It's delightful, to us who are grey at the temples, to see all these young carefree faces about the street.

And it's fine that that old ugly building in Hellihole Road is being put to such good use. It's a great experience to have a talk with the Warden, Bill Wallace of Glasgow—he's great fun and he's very intelligent.

Last night (Sunday) I went to the Royal to have a drink and a talk with Jeremy Rundall, a journalist from *The Sunday Times*, who is writing a book about his travels in the Hebrides, Orkney, Shetland, Faroe, Lapland and Greenland. We checked over together some details in the Orkney chapter: which includes (among other things) a marvellous account of a frontal assault, in snow and sun, of the Ward Hill of Hoy in 1969.

A few lads with the accents of Lowland Scotland greeted us. Jeremy bought them a glass of beer. They drifted away to play darts.

A quartet came in—three girls and a young man smoking a pipe. They were laden with impedimenta. They had just come back from Shetland. They spoke with shining eyes of how sick they had been on the *Orcadia*. Two of the girls were nurses from Glasgow—they hated having to go back on the *St Ola* next morning, but their holiday was almost over. 'Perhaps,' one of them said, 'we'll come back and be nurses in Orkney—that would be wonderful!...'

One of the girls unslung a guitar and began to sing ballads in a sweet clear voice. The darts players drifted over. One of the regulars began to dance in the middle of the floor. Ballad followed ballad—Scottish, Jamaican, Irish.

But it was almost ten o'clock, and time for the shutters to go up.

I spoke outside to the other young man and woman who had been on the Shetland trip. They were going back, they said, to Belfast in the morning...

More and more singers and guitars are crowding into town, to be in good time for Shopping Week, which is becoming more and more a festival of youth; and a good thing too.

The Boys of Summer

20.7.1972

The long narrow sun-splashed street is choked with cars three or four times a day. The town is swarming with tourists from the five continents. In the evening the bars throb and thrum with pop groups. On Friday of last week the first full heat of summer was turned on. In the late evening tongues of sea-haar felt along the hills, promising more heat on the Saturday....

I am trying to remember how a summer day must have been in Stromness in the 1930s—for a boy of a generation ago it was vastly different from today.

It was more restricted, for one thing. You lived in Stromness and in Stromness you stayed, unless by some rare stroke of luck you were taken to the Dounby Show or the Kirkwall Market in Couper's bus. As for a holiday in Aberdeen or Edinburgh, such fabulous adventures were not to be thought of.

In those days the *St Ola*—not the present boat, but a small black narrow vessel—brought only small numbers of visitors to Orkney. They, and the local children, looked at each other with equal curiosity. Sometimes a fine-spoken lady would set up an easel on the street—you could, in those days; there was a slow cautious car only every half-hour or so—and do a watercolour of Melvin Place or Puffer's Close. The small boys thought how strange and exotic the visitors were, like folk from another planet.

As for the boys themselves, they ran all summer long with bare feet on flagstones hot as pancakes. (Or so they dream nowadays, looking back—it is a classic case of how all the bad things are suppressed in the mind—the days of rain and wind and fog.) But certainly those eight weeks of the summer holidays were outside time; there was a sense of boundless freedom; for school was much more of a prison then than it is now.

We fished from the end of piers. The caught sillocks were sold to wives with cats, four for a penny. We bathed from slips, and were so innocent we knew no evil of the sewers that kept spilling into the happy blue water. We drifted across the fields to Warbeth, and rummaged in the pools for whelks, and dared each other to crawl deep into the Miners' Hole, which was said to end somewhere under the farm of Clook...

And on the way home we blew 'clocks' and fought each other with 'soldiers'; while the girls (whom we shunned as if they were an alien race) made daisy chains and held buttercups under each others' chins.

Summer in Stromness was quieter and more innocent in that distant age.

Shopping Week

27.7.1972

It's such a gay, giddy, coloured wheel, Shopping Week, that when it's all over—I write this on the Monday morning following—it's difficult to separate the various incidents.

But I remember the blast of heat on the day before the opening, and the young ones roaming the streets without shirts, and the *Ola* disgorging hundreds more sweating tourists; and, in the evening, the cool beer at The Braes, and a guitar and ballads.

The weather was beautiful. The organisers couldn't have chosen a milder or drier week. (Rain is what they most fear during the week.) The worst weather was the dense hank of fog that blotted out Stromness on Wednesday evening. But I like the fog after a warm day—mysterious, silent, and shapeless—and holding promise of good weather on the next day.

There was something biblical about the crowd on the side of Brinkie's as darkness fell on Thursday evening—the great open-air fire, the beer cans going from mouth to mouth, the delicious chicken, ballad singers somewhere in the distance. In fact, it was such a merry evening that I have only a vague memory of leaving it.

On Friday evening there was a marvellous house-warming party at a house on a pier, with mince-and-tatties and singing. It was a delight to sit in such lovely rooms and talk to old friends. When I went home the dawn was grey-and-gold and scarlet in the east.

The rain threatened all Saturday; threatened, but never fell; at the most there was a thin 'mirr' or 'driv' in the evening, but by that time nobody was caring. The night drove on 'wi sangs and clatter'—the huge kaleidoscope spun faster and faster—the splendid but rather small fancy dress parade went past—the rockets streaked up the sky from the Holms and released showers of golden rain, and silent globes of light, and midnight rainbows...

It seemed to be such a full and busy week. Only next day did it occur to me how many things I had missed—the football matches, the baby show, the yard of ale, etc. So rich is Shopping Week; like a sequence of six Hogmanays.

The Book of Black Arts

3.8.1972

Nobody seems to know anything nowadays about *The Book of Black Arts*: though in my young days all the old men could tell the story in different versions.

Where *The Book* came from originally nobody knows, though one shudders to speculate. It was printed, it seems, on some dark infernal press; and it looked devilish too, with its white ghastly letters on jet-black pages.

The wonderful thing about it, once it was in your possession, was that you could perform supernatural actions; such as jump over houses, or transport yourself from Stromness to Kirkwall in a flash, or draw the virtue of your neighbour's cow into your own cow so that she was fat all the year round with milk and butter and cheese—while the spindly beast next door was led in disgust to the slaughterman...

The horrible thing about *The Book of Black Arts* was that you couldn't get rid of it. You could burn it, tear it in shreds and scatter the pieces to the wind, throw it over the Black Craig. When you came home there the evil thing was, in the cupboard or the desk... The only way you could get rid of it was to sell it to somebody at less than the price you paid for it.

So, a man would have *The Book* for ten years or so—and be the source of much malicious fun in his parish—but then, growing old and smitten in conscience, he would sell it for a shilling—he himself had paid one-and-six for it—to some foolish curious creature at the Dounby Market. He in turn became the clownish wonder-worker of the district, until maybe some sudden illness caused him to wrap it in sacking and sell it in the Smithy for sixpence (after much fearful bargaining).

Eventually—so the story goes—a simple-minded servant lass bought the infernal volume for a farthing; and it seemed she was stuck with it till her dying day; after which her soul would have to bear it down to the fires where it had originated.

But the lass was not so simpleminded after all. Beset with anguish and terror, she carried *The Book* to the minister, Rev Charles Clouston of Sandwick, who solemnly buried the accursed thing in his garden; after which nothing more was ever heard of it.

How did *The Book* come to Orkney in the first place? A foreign ship was wrecked on the Kirk Rocks. The cargo was plundered. Some days after a beachcomber found it among the tangles. (But how he ever managed to read it nobody knows, for the language would have been foreign, probably Latin.)

An old Stromness man first told me the story on a winter night forty years ago. I went home looking over my shoulder from time to time.

A Washout

17.8.1972

Alas, poor Dounby! The second Thursday in August is generally one of the most delightful days in the Orkney calendar. You spend the morning in a tingle of anticipation. Last Thursday, when I peered out after breakfast, the sky was a drift of grey and silver and the paving stones were wet. But when I went to catch the one o'clock bus at the Pier Head, the silver had prevailed—there were even patches of blue in the sky.

All the way to Dounby it kept dry. But the bus had hardly emptied near the Show Park when a fringe of rain went coldly across the village. Two or three of us went into the Smithfield till such time as the sun would break out. (For the sun always shines on the Dounby Show—at least the weather has been good, or tolerable, for the past six or seven years.)

Patrons came into the Smithfield with their coat collars turned up and caps pulled down and backs rainspattered. As always, it is pleasant talking to Orcadians from other islands and parishes at the Dounby Show. (The day has a way of banishing shyness.)

Well, you just can't sit in the Smithfield all day. Outside the road shone and the rain came in swaps and gusts. Gone were the silver and the blue from the sky. It had settled into a real awkward day of rain.

Everything happened awkwardly from then on. There was a queue standing in the rain to get into the Show Park. The lovely animals stood or lay about the field in dejected attitudes. One felt deeply sorry for the organisers and the farmers and all the Dounby folk.

The beer tent was doing extraordinarily good business. Every fresh flurry of rain sent another score under the canvas. The wind rose with the rain, and the marquee billowed like a schooner in the South Atlantic. And still more folk surged in with rain dripping from their noses. The grassy floor was littered with plastic whisky containers and cardboard beer mugs.

By three o'clock I had had enough of the Dounby Show of 1972. By a stroke of good fortune I met some Stromness friends who were bound west in their peedie car. We had coffee and cakes in the Tormiston Mill. It was the first time I had been there, and it's a really good-looking place, and deservedly popular.

The rain kept slashing against the windows of the mill with cold nagging intensity.

Rackwick

24.8.1972

It was near the height of the flood. Angus Brown's boat went into a welter of waves in Hoy Sound, deep-bosomed surges, and the boat rode them with style and enjoyment till we rounded the west Graemsay light and cruised easily towards Hoy.

Through the dark valley we went in a Landrover, till we saw first a glint of sea, then the sombre perpendicular of the Too and the crofts on the high, green, west wall of the valley.

A score of haymakers, young and old, were helping Jack Rendall in the hayfield at Glen Farm, until finally the tractor swayed into the yard with a load of baled hay, and a dozen bairns cheering around. In the evening light the oatfield looked lovely, the tender, aerial, rustling oats thickly starred with charlock.

Though it is only a few miles from Stromness as the crow flies, Rackwick always puts an edge on the appetite. We had a marvellous late supper of curried beef and eggs, and homebrewed ale. And oh, the deep peace of lying in a box bed, with the boom of the sea in your ears!...

But to wake up in a box bed with the sound of rain in the thatch and windows is not so pleasant. When Rackwick weeps, its grief is long and forlorn and utterly desolate. The rain wept in the valley all the next day. You sit inside reading, writing, playing games, eating, conversing, but there is no way of overcoming the incredible desolation of a rainy day in Rackwick.

There was drama next morning. A violent gust came from Moorfea at 8am and blew down one of the tents in the field outside. But the sleepers in the tent managed to move their belongings inside in a short time, and by evening they were laughing at what had happened. The gust was part of the great wind that pushed the rain clouds away. The heart soon recovers its natural cheerfulness at the first sight of a gleam of sunshine. That day we walked all over the valley. Beyond Burnmouth, the burn was in full brown spate after the deluges of yesterday. We climbed among the high ruined crofts, Quernstones, Greups, Scar, as far as Bunertoon[1], incredibly perched on a high ledge above the Atlantic. The sun and the cold wind made walking a pleasure...

This evening I have to return home. It is so pleasant sitting at the sheltered, sun-smitten side of the croft. The old magic of Rackwick is stronger than all its threnodies and desolations.

The First St Magnus Fair

31.8.1972

I never saw such a crowd in Kirkwall as last Wednesday afternoon. We went in by car to the Lammas Fair on the Market Green. The small girl who was with us was very excited, and I added fuel to the

---

1 From 1971 to 1998 the house of Peter Maxwell Davies, composer.

excitement by telling her about swingboats, a Punch and Judy show, and the Lady with the Fish Tail. What she was longing for most of all was to win a coconut. 'How about a goldfish?' I said. But no, she thought it would be impossible to take a goldfish home safely in a car.

So, then, we found ourselves at last in the heart of this dense throng. It was very difficult to get near the stalls for the press of people; but one rejoiced all the same to see the brisk business that was being done. I tend to be panicky and claustrophobic in such a crowd, and so I was glad at last to be out in the comparative peace of Broad Street, where ladies were sitting at small tables in the open air drinking tea.

We longed for ice cream; but the large queue outside the ice cream van clamouring to be cooled down daunted us, and we went instead into the Town Hall to see the excellent St Magnus Exhibition.

Out again in the sunshine, the crowd had thinned somewhat. Here and there one could see famous figures: Jo Grimond, Lord Birsay. Baskets were filled with crabs, turnips, Orkney cheese. Over the Fair loomed the kindly threatened cathedral. I thought to myself, 'This is how it should be, commerce and religion hand-in-glove with one another—the needs of body and soul overtly recognised—the whole man catered for...' Whereas, all too often in recent centuries, the market place and the pen and the church have operated in separate sealed compartments.

It was on the whole a happy heartening day. But the small girl in our company was bitterly disappointed. There were no coconut shies or Punch and Judy or goldfish—all she saw, being less than four feet high, were Orkney feet endlessly rising and falling and shuffling past, a confusion of trousers and skirts round the Market Cross.

In the end she was a bit consoled with ice cream and crisps, and all the way back to Stromness told her teddy bear what had transpired on this famous day... By the time she is old enough to enjoy it, may the annual St Magnus Fair in Kirkwall have its secure place once more in the Orkney summer calendar.

A Car Splurge

21.9.1972

In a brand-new, fern-green Ford Cortina, for the past fortnight, we have traversed every single road in the Mainland, Burray, South Ronaldsay. The weather has been magnificent: rich heraldic skies, the harvest light, and in the fields the symbols of fruition everywhere—stooks of hoarded oats and bere.

Orkney is loveliest of all at this time of year, when she stands, loaded with ripeness, at the door of winter.

There are a score of places I will remember with pleasure in the dark days. We went one afternoon to the modest summit of the Ward Hill in South Ronaldsay; the whole island, from the wreck of the *Irene* to the kirk that keeps the stone with St Magnus's footprints in it, lay under us. Herston, on the south shore of Widewall Bay, is a lovely hamlet. Intending to walk to Hoxa Head, a great black raincloud burst and drenched us. But that new car has everything; its heater had us dry again, coats and hair, by the time we got back to Stromness.

The roads of Orkney form a web of which nearly every strand is beautiful. There is that delightful road that turns from the arrow-straight Rendall road and climbs among crofts and farms; and climbs higher, among moors and peat bogs and a few last lonely crofts; and then you breast the rise and the whole of Harray and Sandwick lies before you, with the gleam of lochs, and Hoy beyond.

You can never lose Hoy on the roads of the West Mainland, except where now and then they dip into hollows or tilt towards the Atlantic. Those noble, lovely shapes haunt Orcadians wherever they go, like immemorial heraldry, and (one must believe) in some sense mould our communal life and outlook.

Another afternoon, having viewed half of Orkney from the top of Ravie Hill (and there too the road winds uphill all the way), we cruised down into the fertile valley of Marwick. Strolling, full-uddered cattle added to the richness of the end of summer. From 'the bay of the mere'—from which the district, it seems, takes its name—we walked southwards to the noust below Howe farm, and the cluster of old boathouses set steeply and enchantingly into the face of the crag.

It had been a warm, bright afternoon. Now it got suddenly overcast, and random drops fell cold on our faces. A few colours and shades were subtracted from the seascape, but it kept the beauty it can never lose. And there against the southern sky stood the Kame of Hoy, and the Old Man keeping watch through a rain-haze on the Atlantic.

Letter-writing

28.9.1972

When one's trade is writing for five days a week, the fact that the sixth day has to be set aside for writing letters seems at best like a busman's holiday, and at worst a burden not to be borne.

Yet the answering of letters is a task that must be tackled coldly and methodically—otherwise one would be drowned under a ceaseless flood of correspondence.

And how awful it would be—I console myself with the thought—if there were no letters to answer. Two of the thrilling times of the day are round about 9.30am and 3pm, when the letterbox rattles and there is the whisper of falling letters in the lobby. The 'south end' postman has come and gone...

But the stack of unanswered letters grows as the week advances, until on Saturday morning the pile is complete. You crush the empty eggshell, you stow cup and saucer and plate away, you sit down grim-faced to the task. And you think, resentfully, 'Why, when I have slaved my guts out all week with pen and paper, should this added burden be put on me?'

Variety eases the load, a little. There is a letter to an intelligent lady CBS producer in Edinburgh; one to a nephew in Stirlingshire; one to the Ministry of Social Security in Kirkwall; another to a talented young writer who is languishing in a bleak, bare garret in Newcastle but will be coming to live in Orkney after New Year; another to a publisher, with the suggested blurb of a new novel...

One good thing; I am so used to writing that the letters flow as if some computer was putting them out! (But I am flesh and blood and no computer.) Letter-writing follows a constant curious graph—first the mind kindles with the sheer mechanical act of writing—a few felicitous phrases rise to the surface—you smile in spite of yourself—after a page or two the friend you are writing to becomes actual and dear by the mere fact of communication, and he ceases to be a remote nuisance that must somehow be silenced with an answer.

That's the way it always happens. You begin the epistolatory task in a black mood, and end always in a kindly glow, as if you had just left a circle of friends.

The Changing Stylus

5.10.1972

I am writing this with one of those ballpoint pens that go like a song.

We all began writing at the age of five in the infant class ruled over kindly but firmly by Miss Matheson. The tools of the trade then were slates in wooden frames and slate pencils. When all the class was hard at it, what tiny squeaks and shrieks filled the room, like fifty mice in agony! Afterwards you rubbed out what you had written with a damp rag. (But some naughty boys spat on the slate and rubbed it dry with the sleeves of their jerseys.)

From slates, at about the age of seven, we graduated to lead pencils and jotters. This wasn't nearly so much fun. But it was nice to own a knife and sharpen your pencil twenty times a day, whether it needed sharpening or not.

A very important day arrived, under the regime of Miss Garson in Standard One—learning how to write with a pen. First the inkwells had to be filled on every desk from a huge stone bottle. Then the new nibs were fitted on the pens and we set to work on our copy books, writing out, in copperplate, proverbs like 'A burnt child dreads the fire' and 'Too many cooks spoil the broth'... What black blots there were on every page! What filthy index fingers! Sometimes there was a minor tragedy—an inkwell would be upset and a black torrent flowed over copy book and trousers and floor. Some pupil was in serious trouble then—his classmates took in the scene with awed delight.

My first fountain-pen was a Platignum that cost one-and-six. I wore it proudly, the first of a long succession of fountain pens, in my breast pocket (and was convinced that the nib was made of platinum—far more precious metal than gold—till I was brutally disillusioned by an older boy).

Some time in the late 1940s the ballpoint arrived on the scene. They made a filthy, smudgy, spiderish mess of every sheet of paper they touched. But somehow they became universally popular. And, slowly, they improved. The smudges were got under control; they no longer leaked in your pocket. As they improved they got cheaper and cheaper. They are one of the few articles to ride the wave of inflation with serene disregard. This one I am writing with now is the most fluent ballpoint I have ever owned.

But I will not boast yet. In a minute or two it is liable to turn temperamental, and only write the second letter of every word, for example. Nothing is so infuriating as that. The fact is that a totally trustworthy writing implement has never yet been devised; except, perhaps, that joy of our infancy—the slate pencil.

Poets Laureate

19.10.1972

So, we have got a new Poet Laureate at last, and one known in Orkney, for he was here a couple of years ago— John Betjeman.

He is not the first Poet Laureate to have visited Orkney either. In the late nineteenth century Alfred Lord Tennyson came to Kirkwall. At once the greatest local honour known was thrust upon him—the Freedom of the City and Royal Burgh, the burgess ticket. Tennyson was a rather morose man; he sat in the choir of the Paterson Kirk wrapped in impenetrable gloom. Fortunately the great Mr Gladstone was there too, and he spoke for both of them—great thunderous rolling periods the like of which Kirkwall has never heard since. The two great pillars of the Victorian establishment were taken, if I remember rightly, as far west as Stenness, to visit Maeshowe and the Standing Stones. But the eye of the Laureate never rested on Stromness and so was lost the possibility of another immortal lyric.

The Poets Laureate have, in general, been a dreary, ridiculous lot: Nahum Tait, Colley Cibber, Robert Southey, Shadwell, and the greatest clown of all, Tennyson's successor in the post, Sir Alfred Austin. He wrote, among other peerless gems, this couplet about the appendectomy of King Edward VII:

Through the wires the electric message came,
'He is no better, he is much the same.'

There are two reasons why poets do not fall over each other to grasp the laurel branch. The first is that the laurel branch has sat so often on asinine heads. The second is that the wages are poor—£100 a year, I think, and a butt of malmsey wine. (I think the wine barrel has lately been translated, like so much more that is touching and archaic, into terms of money.)

But it must not be forgotten, all the same, that a few very great men have borne the title. The first one of all, Shakespeare's friend, Ben Jonson, was no mean figure. But then there was that long procession of nonentities till a very great poet, Wordsworth, took over from Robert Southey. When Wordsworth died in 1850—a very old man, a spent volcano, having used up all his glory and passion in youth—another great poet followed him, the same Lord Tennyson who sat in gloomy silence in the Paterson Kirk. I have thousands of Tennyson's lines in my mind. I never see the full power of the ebb in Hoy Sound without remembering this:

But such a tide as moving seems asleep,
  Too full for sound or foam,
When that which drew from out the boundless deep
  Turns again home...

As for the twentieth-century Laureates—Bridges, Masefield, Day Lewis—they have been neither great nor negligible, but in the middle of the road, honest probing craftsmen who have produced the occasional masterpiece. The latest in the line, John Betjeman, promises to be the same. He is a great admirer of Tennyson, and he makes, with fine craftsmanship, the same kind of verbal music.

The Public Library

26.10.1972

Stromnessians, it seems, are not making full use of their library. The number of borrowers is only about half of Kirkwall's. It is not that the folk in the west are more uncultured than their fellow-Orcadians; but perhaps over the decades they have fallen out of the habit of reading.

Nowadays there are powerful enemies of the book abroad. The chief of these is television. How easy it is, in the evening after the day's work, to sit back in the armchair and let the facile images flood through the mind. Another enemy is the newspaper. Instant sensation—the separation of everything into black and white; that is much more soothing than having to reflect upon what Bernard Shaw, or H. G. Wells, or even Zane Grey, meant by putting it in such a way.

But in just the same way as we go for a walk before supper, to tone the system up and to sleep better, so it is always a good thing to give the mind a little exercise; or bit by bit it will wither—it will accept anything and everything it is told—it will be soil ripe for the dictator or the super-bureaucrat.

Therefore we ought to cherish our library at the foot of Hellihole, which was presented to the town by Mrs Marjorie Skea of Corrigall in the year 1904.

The Stromness Library has never been in better shape, or so well stocked, as it is today. Recently it was enlarged by the taking over of a large part of the old gloomy reading-room, and now it is a delight to wander among the thousands of books available to us. (The reading-room, too, is much the better for being made small and intimate.)

Furthermore a great treasure of old Orkney books is about to be made available to Stromness readers. This is made up in large measure of the Garson collection, bequeathed to the town in 1928. Theoretically, of course, it was always possible to consult these local books by requesting permission, but in actual fact hardly a soul did so. They remained shut up in their great locked bookcase prison. But soon the Garson collection is to be removed downstairs into the main library, and now that there is such an interest in Orkney's past, there's no doubt that that treasury will be made full use of. We should think ourselves lucky with our new-look library. The first library came to Stromness in 1819, but it seems not to have been serious enough for the city fathers, for, in the words of the *New Statistical Account* (1842)—'For some years past, novels have been excluded, and works of a more solid character substituted in their place. The annual subscription is seven shillings...'

A Hidden Treasure

2.11.1972

There was once an Orkneyman who had a small croft between the hill and the sea. Jock was by no means wealthy, and he never could be. But he liked his work, and he liked to sit at his door in the evening and just look at the sea and the sky. His wife Maggie kept a fine garden at the front, with daffodils and tulips growing in their season, and there was a useful gooseberry bush and a lovely rose bush. Jock liked nothing better than to walk about in the garden smoking his pipe at sunset...

One evening he bent and picked up a small round heavy pebble. He had never seen anything like it before. It was not an ordinary stone. The thing lay rich and heavy in his palm. A qualm of foreboding went through him. He took it into the house and he hid it away in a drawer, and he never mentioned it to a soul, not even to Maggie or to peedie Tom, until the day of his death; which was twenty useful and contented years later.

The day after the funeral Tom was going through his father's papers and possessions—not an onerous task by any means—when he came on the pebble lying in the drawer beside the big family bible.

Tom weighed the stone in his hand. He looked at it for a long time, his head askew with the wildest of speculations. He had an impulse—in the midst of his long consideration—to throw the thing into the sea. Instead, he booked a plane seat to London and took the stone to a famous jeweller there.

Tom in his own way, and with his forward-looking nature, was as happy a man as his father had been. He had more of this world's goods; he had for example a car and a TV set. His wife was a pleasant girl too, though she no longer baked bannocks or made gooseberry jam. They both believed, without ever having to mention it, that progress would make life better and smoother for everyone for ever and ever to the end of time. They wished, like everybody else, that they had more money, in order fully to enjoy the fruits of progress. They were saving up for the first baby, and for a colour TV set, and for a new car. They liked their little croft almost as much as old Jock and Maggie had done.

The pebble was given and taken in a London shop.

Things happened fast after that. The rosebush was uprooted. The cottage and outhouses were levelled. A shaft was sunk where the oatfield had been. Men probed and quarried for diamonds. (I will not speak of noise and dust and fumes, for fear of being thought to influence in a certain way the balance of the parable.)

As for Tom and his wife and son, I cannot say whether they are happier or not. They are certainly changed. Their sea and sky are not what they were...

The Orcadian, with his heritage all round him, is balancing in the palm of his hand at this moment something incalculable and exotic. Will he be able to hold on to both the old and the new? Or will he in the end lose both? Or will he have to choose between the one and the other?

He has only a few days left for decision.

Guy Fawkes Day

9.11.1972

I have been trying to write letters all this morning (Saturday) to a background of continual knockings at the door. And then, when I went, there was a cluster of apple-cheeked bairns, with carved and painted turnips on sticks, chanting 'A penny to burn me pop'.

Fortunately I had remembered at the week's beginning that the 5th of November was looming up, and so I kept all my small change and hoarded it on the sideboard against the morning of the procession of turnips; remembering that once upon a time I was a small boy and took part in the ritual.

'A penny to burn me pop'—Bless our hearts, we didn't for one moment know what the slogan meant. All we knew was that we had to pinch a turnip out of a farmer's field and take it home, about the 3rd of November. Then our fathers or our elder brother would sculpt the turnips with the kitchen carving knife. Buttons for eyes, broken matches for teeth, splashes of vermilion on cheeks and nose; and a stick to carry it round with. Then we were ready to take part in the dance.

At the end of the day we might have as much as four shillings or five shillings; our trouser pockets bulged with a huge freight of copper.

Then, under the gas lamps, the splurge. Sweeties, chocolate, ice cream, lemonade. But, after the inevitable sickness, there was generally one tangible trophy left in the morning. All the boys bought torches to light them through the winter: squat shapes with a lens like a huge frog's eye. The streets and closes were full of beams and flickers.

...After a week or two the batteries gave out, and of course we had no more money to renew them; and the torches rusted away all winter in the kitchen drawer.

'A penny to burn me pop.' Nowhere else in the world but in Stromness is that slogan chanted. I wonder in what bigoted religious brain, some time in the mid-nineteenth century, the phrase first took root, and was passed on to the innocent-mouthed children.

I happen to have a high regard for that good austere lonely man in the Vatican—but I give pennies to the children when they come to the door with their carved turnips—for I'm sure that he, if he knew about it, would also smile and bless the innocent mouths.

'One Foot in Eden...'

16.11.1972

How disappointed the young American was! He didn't say anything, of course, but I could see betrayal on his face. Way back home, in the winter, he had read an Orkney story; and happening to be in Britain on a crash holiday, he whizzed north to see if the place was really like it said in the book. Who better to go to than the source from which the story had come? So, he knocks on this door. And five seconds later—having been ushered inside—the look of betrayal exploded across his innocent face.

What he was expecting, of course, was a wee croft in the middle of the moorland. There would be a few hens clucking round the door, and a water barrel at the end of the house. Maybe a goat tethered on the 'blasted heath', and a black-and-white collie barking a welcome. Then, inside, the lovely smell of peats burning, and old-style ale brewing in the kirn, and straw-backed chairs, and bacon curing in the rafters, and sillocks curing in the chimney smoke.

But this—a new council house, and most of the things that progress lavishes on her children—TV, electric fire, transistor, a spread of gaudy rugs everywhere! We conversed politely for ten minutes or a quarter of an hour, and smiled and nodded, but the look of disappointment did not fade... He went away, a sadder but a wiser man...

The first wild storm of winter flung itself at us on Monday last, and has gone on, raging and scratching, for most of the week. After that long golden autumn—the mellowest that anyone remembers—we had forgotten how fierce our weather can be once the web of darkness thickens about us. So, I was glad of my electric fire, and my transistor, and my hot water bottle, as the smart new council house shuddered under the gale and the sleet. Hypocrite or not, I give half a genuflection in the direction of the goddess Progress (the worship of which has been the true religion of Orkney for the past century).

But the old Orkney crofts, built low and snug into the hillside, sailed on serenely through the storms of winter, generation after generation. The peatstack never failed, the paraffin lamp burned on, the back numbers of the *Christian Herald* (smelling deliciously of smoke) were there on the window ledge to read. The well was full. The cattle were safe in the byre.

The young American was right: I had exchanged ancient tranquillity for gilt and tinsel. But most of us have come so far away from that poor earth-rooted beautiful way of life that to go back would be more painful than to struggle on into the age of the Atom... What is important is never to forget the unique place where we started.

The Day-spring

23.11.1972

These winter mornings, bed is a great attraction. How delightful to wake up in that warm, magical cave! You could stay there forever, except that somewhere deep inside you the stern, small voice of duty is calling. In my position, not having to present myself to some boss at 9am, the temptation to bide on in the magic cave can be over-whelming. But the voice of duty spoils everything—it shatters every luxury, every delicious dream. With a stupendous effort of the will you throw aside the blankets, put your feet on the cold mat, struggle into chilly clothes.

The house is a hollow iceberg. The first thing to do, in the kitchen, is to switch on the fan-heater, full blast. Then the transistor, for the nine o'clock news. Then the cold water tap, for the breakfast tea (which is the most delicious tea of the day, by far). Then the cooker ring for the toast and the boiled egg. Tides of warmth are beginning to swirl all over the kitchen.

...9.05am—'a religious service for primary schools'... A twirl of the knob, and you are listening to Bach, or Kodaly, and kidding yourself that you are enjoying it.

Sometimes you get so absorbed in the rituals of breakfast that you forget to make signals to the world that you are alive and well—such as, unlock the door, take in the milk, draw back the curtains in the living room.

One morning a while ago I was so engrossed in a certain piece of work after breakfast that the curtains above the street remained closed. About noon a vigilant friend entered cautiously, to see if I was still alive. At least, he reasoned, I must be on a bed of sickness. Not at all—it was just that I had been caught up in a full flush of work...

When the second mug of tea has been drained to the dregs, you get all snobby and superior, thinking of all the shameless creatures still lying in their beds: unwilling to leave that womb, bourne of all life, for the stern business of the day. What would the world be, if it was full of such slugabeds! (Forgetting what the world of the nine o'clock news was like: Ulster, letter bombs, Vietnam, mugging...)

But anyway, feeling virtuous and superior and warm, you put away the breakfast dishes, and set sheets of paper beside you, and click your biro into the ready position: and another winter day in this stern world of getting and spending is about to begin.

A Winter Week

30.11.1972

SUNDAY: Ian Grimble has in the past two winters become one of television's best serious entertainers. He has been first rate for several weeks on the history of Stuart Scotland. Today it was Knox and Mary, Queen of Scots. There are still a few mouths that call her 'murdress', 'adultress'. But, the poor young princess, coming from the high courtliness and gaiety and poetry of France, among all these violent fanatics! No wonder she drowned slowly in a cold and bitter sea... I hope the BBC don't let Ian Grimble go in a hurry.

MONDAY: 'Please,' said the publisher's editor, 'write us a ghost story'... What a fraud I am—I've never seen a ghost in my life—but your hack is prepared to write about anything. So, I sat down and wrote about an Orkney ghost who thought he was still alive; but of course he got quickly and brutally disillusioned when he moved, invisible and still hungry for approval, among his folk; and heard what they had to say about him!... I wrote it in one hectic rush. And was oh! so pleased with myself... Then, later, I reread it, and the moment of truth dawned. It was a dreadful piece of work. Well, not entirely. Something may be salved from the wreckage...

TUESDAY: They say nearly everybody in Orkney gets rheumatism sooner or later. The dampness penetrates to the marrow of every bone. For a fortnight I have had a sore thumb, with some swelling. It isn't disabling, except when I try to lift the teapot or turn the tap with my left hand—then the whole arm blossoms with pain to the shoulder... There is this constant gnaw and nag. I hope it soon goes away.

WEDNESDAY: The making of ale is a queer business. I can never come to grips with the time factor. During the summer, the period of fermentation was three or four days, and that was fine—it meant you could drink the stuff the same week that you made it... But this brew that stands in the corner of my kitchen, it has been there for eight days now. It is a dark, quiet tarn in the mornings. 'Ah,' you say, 'time for bottling.' By mid-afternoon, there is a gentle seethe in it, a new lacing of foam. I will not be bottling today—I don't want my precious bottles burst.

THURSDAY: Work all morning at the story. The ghost is beginning to emerge as a dark, piteous, suffering essence. I think, if a bit of melodrama here and there is toned down, that it may work out. The moral is never to despair—there's always something to be plucked out of disaster.

The brew is still showing faint signs of life.

Rev Ian Paisley on John Knox on TV in the evening. Neither the one nor the other attracts me. But Mr Paisley, give him his due, is another superb TV entertainer.

FRIDAY: A new publication out today from Charles Senior, Stromness, who keeps the first-rate bookshop: *Orkney Birds* by E. Balfour. The cover, a drawing of a hen-harrier by William Senior (the publisher's brother, a frequent visitor to Orkney) is very striking... I hope Stromness Books and Prints will do more publishing of Orkney items in the future.

The story has improved. It will do. So will the ale. Tonight I bottled seven gallons—a weary task, with buckets, jugs, and spillings, but one does it with a song in the heart!

The Snows of Christmas

7.12.1972

December already—how quickly the months pass—only three weeks to the shortest day, the solstice. It is a sign of age, no doubt, that one dreads winter and muffles oneself in woollens and warmth till the first snowdrops of spring appear. The poet Yeats said it was the growing weariness with life itself—ageing, we even tire of summer and harvest.

December for a child is a marvellous magical month. He exists then and then only among the stars and the storms and the snow, without hindsight or foresight.

He writes—or used to write, in my boyhood—long letters to a man in a red coat in Lapland. *Deer Santa, I want a train and sweeties and a ball for playing football also a game of drafts and appel and orang.* It didn't matter, in the event, that all I got was the ball, the sweets and the fruit—the joy of Christmas morning and the loaded stocking at the end of the bed was like no other joy.

Life, you might think, looking back, must be a cheat and a disappointment for a child. For all the Christmas stories and carols and illustrations are laden with snow—and yet most of my early Decembers had nothing but rain and wind and darkness. But, really, it did not matter. In the world of the imagination, where a child lives half his time, there was always snow in December—the whole world hung sideways with its marvellous white burden. On the rare occasions when imagination meshed with reality, and the snow made Orkney a few silver humps in the midst of piercing blues, then the whole child—body and spirit—was touched with a rare sweet wild ecstasy.

Snowballs, snowmen, the sledges hurtling down Hellihole—there was no end to it—it seemed to go on for ever...

Time is unkind to us all. I remember a snowfall two winters ago. It came about breakfast time, one huge whirling blizzard, and afterwards Stromness was a transfigured place. And yet when I went to the town for my messages that afternoon, person after person I met kept saying, 'O, isn't this terrible!'...'O, what a dreadful day!' The rare beauty—so suddenly come, so quickly to go—had, it seemed, touched them not at all; and on a day when we should all have been rejoicing creatures in a new pure place...

When, after a few years, we children got to understand that there were certain doubts about that old, kind man from Lapland in the red coat, Santa Claus still went on living for a long time in the imagination. He still does, in a way.

Beware only of the December when you say, 'What nonsense! Santa Claus indeed! It's high time children were told the truth!'... For that will be the same December that the snow will turn into cold, disagreeable, rheumatic-bearing stuff; and another bit of magic will have gone out of life and time.

Sweetie Shops

14.12.1972

The briefest perusal of George S. Robertson's *History of Stromness 1900-1972* shows what a host of peedie shops have closed down during the century. I arrived on the scene towards the end of the first quarter of the century, and having a sweet tooth from earliest infancy, the shops I remember best are the sweetie shops.

Pocket money, to begin with, was one ha'penny a week. Every Friday, aged four or five, I went into Peter Esson's tailor shop at the foot of the Church Road where my father sat, sewing away at the bench.

Peter and Willie Esson and my father pretended not to know what I had come for. They looked quizzically over their spectacles.

'Me pension,' I said—'I've come for me pension...'

Gravely the ha'penny was handed over. 'And see,' said my father, 'that you don't spend it all in one shop.'

Then once more the machine stuttered and scissors clashed and the damp pressing cloth hissed and smoked under the goose; and I was free to go.

A ha'penny in 1926 unlocked the door into endless delights—a lucky bag, a sweet potato (with a ring hidden in the heart of it), a liquorice strap, a sherbet dab...

The shop I knew at the beginning was Janetta Sinclair's (just across the street from Peter Esson's, and in the shadow of the Free Kirk). Janetta had in her window a gigantic clay pipe; and we children used to wonder for hours what legendary hero, if any, ever smoked it.

But after a while the family moved from that neighbourhood to Melvin Place. The nearest sweetie shop was at the foot of Hellihole and was kept by Miss Black, a gentle kind old lady who—all we bairns agreed—gave us good value for our money. The pandrops, or the conversation sweeties, or the butter-nuts that Miss Black seemed to specialise in were emptied out of the scale not into a poke but into a paper screw, and so we sucked and dissolved and crunched the delicious hours away.

And—I might add—rotted our teeth. There was no school dentist in those days. Toothache was the chief disease of childhood. We suffered fiendish agonies twice a year or so. I suppose you could call us martyrs to the bar of toffee.

And there were other magical caves—for example, Ma Cooper's in the steepest part of Dundas Street. You pushed the door open—the bell pinged brightly—you stood in darkness and fragrance. Presently Ma Cooper entered from sweeping her kitchen or feeding her cat; and among the jars of black-striped balls and Sharp's toffee (twopence a quarter) serious negotiations began.

A Ship's Name

23.12.1972

The *St Ola* and Stromness—ship and town are intimately bound up with each other. One without the other is almost inconceivable.

The first *St Ola* of the twenties was that black swan—so frail you thought it could never endure for long the furies of the Pentland Firth. But it endured them for sixty years. I crossed over on her at the age of five, and was sick all the way. But neither I, nor any other Stromnessian given to mal de mer, bore her any grudge. Nor, I think, did we have anything of what is loosely called 'affection' for her. She was simply there, going and coming regularly, a part of our lives like Brinkie's Brae or the Point of Ness.

Nowadays she might be thought of as an ugly old tub, but she was written about more than most boats—Bernard Shaw, H. V. Morton, Eric Linklater (to name but a few) all had interesting things to say about her and her handsome master, Capt Swanson, and her cheerful hardworking obliging crew.

The annals of the present *St Ola* are briefer (1950-74) but the story is the same, substantially, Capt Banks and Capt Stevenson and their men have been worthy successors.

That was why all we Stromnessians read with such interest in last week's *Orcadian* about the new boat that is soon to be built for the Pentland crossing. Said the writer of the article: '...it is strongly hoped that tradition will be maintained by calling her also *St Ola*...'

I wish to put forward a plea for the name to be changed, slightly. For the hallowed name is in fact a Victorian aberration. There never was —*pace* the parish and the hotel in Kirkwall—a Saint Ola. If you think about it coldly it suggests some simpering Scandinavian virgin half-glimpsed through the mists of medieval hagiography. She never existed.

There was, however, a Saint Olaf (of which the present name is a corruption)—a marvellous splendid golden-voiced hero. One can imagine such a one smashing his way in a longship through the Pentland Firth in winter. Any boat should be proud to bear his name.

My frail hope is that the company will seriously consider calling the as-yet-unbuilt ship *St Olaf*; remembering always that, in fact, the second or third mail-boat on the Pentland route was indeed called *Saint Olaf*.

A Quiet Street

4.1.1973

Sitting at the window of this house, on a dull afternoon between Christmas and Hogmanay, everything is quiet and monochrome. The first lights appear in this house and that. A solitary walker goes either north or south. The fishing boats and dinghies are hauled up the noust under my window.

I live in the very quietest part of the street.

And yet it was not always so. Mayburn Court occupies the site of the distillery where Macpherson Brothers made two famous brands of whisky, 'Old Orkney' and 'Old Man of Hoy'. There are still a few bottles in existence; by now they must be liquid gold...

Once, seventy years ago, there was a great trundling of barrels and hogsheads in the courtyard, and the tramp of horses, and from time to time the discreet arrival of the exciseman.

Not only the distillery kept life astir here. Just below me, where the Museum is now, was the Town Hall, the civic heart of Stromness. where the bearded councillors met once a month in solemn assembly; and where from time to time justice was meted out by the bailies.

A few yards along the street was the Police Station with its solitary constable, and cells for the incarceration of rowdy herring-fishers. Again a few yards, and in the corner of Alfred Square was the customs office. Again a few yards, and the Post Office flourished at the turn of the century under a lady called Mrs Ross. In the other direction, within a stone's throw of my window, was Login's Hotel. The street petered out there, but beyond was Stanger's Boatyard (that built the early Pentland Firth mail vessels) and the large farm of Ness (where the golf course now is).

The South End must have been a busy place a century ago. But—I suppose after the Pier was built—the centre of gravity moved northwards, and there most of the business of the town is conducted nowadays.

But this part of Stromness keeps, perhaps more than any other street, the atmosphere of the old town.

I can see from the window, in these last days of 1972, the stretch of water where Gow's pirate ship anchored in 1725, and, beyond, the lovely skyline of Orphir. Will it still be the same, we ask with some foreboding, as the siren of the lighthouse ship *Pole Star* announces the start of, say, 1984?

Come to Lovely Orkney

11.1.1973

I always look forward to reading my Sunday paper on Monday afternoon. But in recent weeks, in the very depths of winter, it has been crowded with holiday articles and advertisements, all sun-splashed and lyrical: people lounging on beaches, splashing in dazzling blue seas, drinking in deck-chairs on ocean liners. All meant, no doubt, to make the shrunken hearts of men rejoice—but there is a bit too much of it—and, anyway, there's a lot to be said for the glories of winter.

It may be that there have been adverts about Orkney, but if so I've missed them. What could we say to lure folk away from the Costa Brava and the Bahamas and the Channel Isles? 'Visit Kirkwall with its lovely rose-red Cathedral and its age-old game of Ba' '... 'Fish your breakfast from one of the twenty piers of Hamnavoe'... 'The coral sand and dazzling lighthouses of Graemsay'... 'South Ronaldsay, Burray, Lamb Holm, Glimps Holm: the islands that Churchill united'... 'Finstown—the village an Irish soldier brogued into being'... 'Where three parishes meet—Dounby, Orkney's Agricultural Heart'... 'Come to Stenness—immerse yourself in the timeless mystery of Maeshowe and Brodgar'... 'Eynhallow—the isle that rose up out of the Sea'... 'There are miles of sun-smitten beaches on Sanday'...

There is no end to the number and variety of slogans that could be shouted abroad about Orkney, so that some little clerk in London or grocer in Glasgow, reading his Sunday paper beside the fire some January afternoon, could feel that death was not so inevitable as it

OTTAKAR'S
a love for books

The Edinburgh Bookshop
57 George Street
Edinburgh,EH2 2JQ
0131 225 4495
george.street@ottakars.co.uk

SALE
27   3 138357   17 Jun 2005 13:01

CASHIER: JULIA
9781904246015 LETTERS FROM HA   7.50

TOTAL   ITEMS   1   7.50

National BookTok   8.00
CHANGE Cash   0.50-

Head Office: St John's House,
72 St John's Road, London, SW11 1PT

Vat No: 561997200
Company Reg No: 2133199

seemed, that the world would suddenly grow young again if he were to book a plane ticket to Orkney in June or July...

But the sad thing is that such a one might be disappointed. There are no beaches here where you can grow as brown as a nut through long sun-drenched weeks. There are no amusement arcades where one can wander in a daze of noise and novelties.

There is magic in Orkney indeed in summer, but it is not the kind of magic that can be caught in holiday brochures, even with the help of coloured photographs. The essence of Orkney's magic is silence, loneliness, and the deep marvellous rhythms of sea and land, darkness and light.

A Burns-tide Speculation

18.1.1973

There was once a family of crofters in the island of Sanday. The time came when it was thought proper for every family to have a surname; and so this particular family took the name of the district they lived in, which was Burness. (This was not unusual—the same was happening with families all over Orkney: the Isbisters, the Hourstons, the Linklaters, the Heddles, the Stoves, etc.)

The Burness family went on living and toiling in Sanday, through middling times and bad (peasants could hardly expect, things being what they were, to have good times, ever). But one or two years in the early seventeenth century, when Earl Patrick crowed from his heraldic dunghill, were particularly bad; and so a venturesome Burness decided to seek his fortune elsewhere than in the scourged and trodden islands of his birth.

He got a passage across the Pentland Firth in a fishing boat, this Burness. He worked for a few years for a Caithness farmer: but in those moorlands also were much distress and oppression, and so the young man set his face towards the south. He had heard that there was a town called Aberdeen, where there was fishing and trading and marketing. He tried his hand at this and that—for he was an adventurous youth—and had great difficulty, to begin with, in comprehending the speech of the north-east, where every syllable was like a chunk of granite: very different from the soft, slow lilt of the islands he had turned his back on. And yet, once he grasped the new music of this language, he felt that it expressed, like no other dialect, the true soul of Scotland.

At last he married, and settled down as a farm-servant in Kincardineshire; and a new generation of Burnesses ploughed the fields and herded the cattle and told stories on a winter night—and another generation came—and then another. All they had, in the midst of their perennial poverty, was the stubborn gaiety of the peasant, the love of language, the delight in character and legend...

* * *

How marvellous it would be if we could prove such a lineage for the poet Burns—if we could trace his beginnings to some forgotten mound in the island of Sanday.

Some have claimed that such may well be the case; and they base their argument on the surname. (The poet's father spelt his name Burness.) Alas, that is the only evidence. It is a very frail shred, and in the Court of Parnassus it would carry no weight at all... And of course it doesn't really matter in the slightest; but still the imagination loves to weave marvellous things from every windblown gossamer thread.

The Kitchen

25.1.1973

Six years ago the present writer could hardly boil an egg, or make a pot of tea.

It's marvellous how necessity can bring out small talents in all of us, that we never thought we had.

Nowadays I can keep myself alive on my own cooking. Not only that, but I even enjoy the food. And the labour entailed, instead of weighing heavily, is a positive joy.

So, when strangers ask me what kinds of tinned foods I especially relish, I make the crushing rejoinder that I rarely open tins—I am my own chef, with a pleasant but limited repertoire. And I don't mean the frying pan either—though there are worse tastes in the world than fried kipper, or ham-and-eggs, or sausages, or mushrooms from the Black Craig.

The making of soup is endlessly interesting, because no two soups ever taste the same. One can experiment, in the silence and loneliness of one's own kitchen. For example, I have come to discover that onions should be put whole into the stock, and not mercilessly chopped up. And you save a lot of electricity by boiling the potatoes whole in the soup. They come out penetrated through and through with succulence and nourishment, to eat along with the beef or the mutton.

Enough soup is made to last two days—sometimes even three, in cold winter weather. On the third morning, what a marvellous thick potage adheres to the bottom of the pot; for soup, like home-brewed ale, improves with keeping. (Though not, of course, beyond the third day.)

The pleasure of making stew (for one) is as great. You do not have to waste time cutting the meat up into many portions, as must be done in families, to save fighting at dinner-time; the whole half-pound goes in, to fry and sizzle and brown for a while. Water is all right for stewing, but a cupful of home-brew is much better. And again, whole onions and potatoes; after a couple of hours you have a feast fit for a ploughman or a prince.

Soup and stew—these for the most part keep me alive. But I go in for occasional luxuries, like grilled steak (though that isn't so much fun to make). Two days ago I tried a staple diet of our ancestors, salt herring and tatties—it was magnificent, and gave me a heroic thirst for the evening's ale...

The repertoire is limited, and might, I admit, grow tiresome over the years. But I have kind friends who invite me to their tables at the weekends, and sometimes during the week; and there I taste the magnificent roast beefs and curries and gammons that my feeble culinary powers could never encompass.

The First Wheelbarrow

1.2.1973

The street shrieked and shrilled—the cobblestones thundered. Nobody in Stromness had heard the like before. People came to their doors. The shopkeeper stopped serving and the customer stopped buying; the cat leapt down from the sack of barley.

Every doorway along the street had three or four gaping, gowping faces.

What they saw was one of their townsmen pushing a contraption in front of him, a slatted thing with handles and legs and metal wheels in front. It was the wheels over the stone that made the unholy noise. Occasionally a spark flew. Small boys ran in panic out of the way.

Old wives in the doorways 'tut-tut-tutted'. Grave merchants stroked their beards. Girls with long skirts put their fingers over their mouths.

The wheels crashed on south over the flagstones, and turned in at a certain grocer's shop; and there, outside a window with salt fish and coffee and an immense cheese and glittering spades in it, the handles were let down lightly.

That was the way the first wheelbarrow came to Stromness, a century ago.

I do not say it was the first wheel to roll through the town. Smart gigs containing important farmers or Kirkwall merchants or the county folk ('the quality') had from time to time gone trotting past the Pier and the Plainstones till they came to the steps in the steep part of the street (not called, still, Dundas Street or Porteous's Brae) and there the blur of wheels had stilled to a stylish set of spokes and varnished wooden circles.

What is the wheel but an inspired abstraction from the sphere? Small boys had rolled stone balls from the beach along the road when Stromness was only a scatter of houses under the granite hill...

I remember a famous raconteur, the late Mr Robert Towers of Graham Place, telling the Stromness Life Boys, forty years ago, the story of how the first wheelbarrow came to Stromness. We small boys were all fascinated. But who the merchant was who brought it from the south

I cannot remember. One old local body, said Mr Towers, thought it was some new kind of machine...

If only those nineteenth-century Stromnessians knew about the multiplicity of wheels that make life in the town of their descendants so hideous!

The English Flu

15.2.1973

Hardly a winter passes but that old subtle enemy of man, flu attacks us from one corner of the globe or another.

This year it is 'the English flu', and no doubt the Scottish Nationalists are saying that it is a typical gift to come from that airt.

It starts—or at least it did in my case—like a mild hangover. But a hangover after two late-night pints of ale—that was impossible... The faint malaise continued all day. Wind searched to the bone—one could not get close enough to the electric fire.

The 'hangover' was much worse next day. Food was eaten, but not relished. There was writing to be done—Orkney legends for children—but that was not to be thought of: the creative faculty was paralysed. Instead I wrote a pile of letters, for that is the easiest kind of writing, and it keeps your mind off things: the headache, the increasing inertia, the shiverings and the burnings, a world drained of all colour and delight.

What does the good old-fashioned Orkneyman do, in such circumstances?—for of course one does not send for the doctor too soon, he being a reminder of our latter end and the tombstone.

The old-fashioned Orkneyman has a good stiff toddy before bedtime. Surely the pure, rich essence of the barley will exorcise the dark spirit that has come to haunt the body's serene cloisters.

So I had a generous toddy (or grog, for I thought that rum would make a pleasant change). It was marvellous while it lasted. For half an hour life was all calypsos and pirates and Spanish gold.

But in the morning the dark spirit had resumed control, with all the former symptoms, plus dry throat... It was high time then to implore the gifts of remedial science.

The Sledges

22.2.1973

The first snow for two winters has come to the islands, and is reluctant to go away.

The sun comes sklintering off the snow in the gardens, and fills my writing-room with such intolerable brilliance that I have to go upstairs to the north-facing room to concentrate properly on the bits of Orkney legend I am trying to write.

But where are the sledges? Where are the clogs? Where are the snowmen?

One grows old, and forgets. But I swear there seem to be far fewer snow vehicles than there used to be forty years ago.

Then Hellihole was a clamorous white highway. It carried a great traffic of sledges, from the humble nails-and-boards to the swift streamlined things with steering-gear and varnish.

The town boys, with cheeks like apples and smoking breath, dragged their sledges halfway to Oglaby, a wearisome trudge: all for the superb thrill of the descent. It never lasted more than a minute. It finished below the library, on Dundas Street. How no brains got bashed out against the stone walls on each side of Hellihole I will never know, for on that frictionless slope there was little room for manoeuvre.

Even at night, under the stars, the Hellihole sledges kept at it.

The old folk sitting beside their fires reading the *People's Journal* would hear till bedtime the thunder and rush of the descending sledges, and the high shivering cries (to which snow, like the sea, gives a special clarity), and the slow thump-thump of sledges being dragged up once more to the starting place.

I was thinking of all these things the other afternoon, in Dundas Street, and had just said to myself, 'Well, of course that sport is impossible now in Hellihole, for the traffic'... when there was a rush and scurry at the corner of the old Subscription School and a sledge flashed like an arrow towards the street. There two boys, shouting and apple-cheeked, abandoned sledge, and prepared for the long haul to the top.

Celtic

1.3.1973

Saturday evening, and snow outside, and the football results beginning to trickle through. Sure enough, Celtic are through to the last eight of the Scottish Cup.

I first heard the magic name Celtic at the age of seven or eight, and for no reason at all gave them my wholehearted allegiance.

Celtic were giants in those days: or at least, like the twin hills of Hoy, they shared the horizon with Rangers. It was a strange season that one or other of them did not win the League or the Cup—usually they shared the honours between them.

Celtic had legendary footballers playing for them. In goal was one of the greatest of all keepers—John Thomson. He died the way a hero should die, in action on the field, and the enemy that tragic Saturday afternoon was the mighty Rangers. John Thomson went down to save a certain goal, and his skull was breached, and he died the same night.

It happened before the days of wireless—we heard, awed and shocked, the news read out of a newspaper by the old folk on the Monday following.

The centre-forward was almost as famous—Jimmy McGrory, and from his head goals flashed into the net as easily as from his powerful feet. And there were McGonagle, and McStay, and Napier...

But then something happened to Celtic—the gods turned their faces away. For nearly a quarter of a century the team struggled on from season to season, achieving none of the famous victories of their predecessors: at best, only an isolated honour now and then. Nothing remained but the magic of the name, and the glamour of green-and-white.

Then, in a short while, Celtic rose out of the trough on to the crest. The man who performed the miracle was an old Celtic player, Jock Stein. Who can ever forget that May evening in Lisbon in 1967, when Celtic took the European Cup with a majestic victory over Inter-Milan?

In the primary classroom in the late 1920s, all the boys had their favourite team. Our small group even had a weekly magazine, with stories, jokes, and crosswords. It was laboriously copied by hand, in ink, and, of course, it was called *The Celt*. I still have the fragment of one copy lying in a cupboard somewhere.

One can never forget one's earliest affections. That is why today, with greying hair, I could still feel a spark of excitement that another victory had come the way of Celtic.

Helen Waters

8.3.1973

An Orkney farmer's daughter called Helen Waters was betrothed to a neighbouring farmer's son called Henry Stewart.

In those days (it seems) the bridegroom in person had to ride round with the 'bids' to the wedding. Some of the guests lived in Hoy; so Henry had to cross the Sound. He took his gun with him for a day's shooting.

He did not come back that evening, or the next day, or the day following. Meantime the wedding ale had been brewed and the bride's dress made, and the first guest had arrived from the North Isles. And the minister in the manse was looking up a suitable text and admonition.

What could be keeping the bridegroom on Hoy? The ducks and hens had been slaughtered. The barn was swept out.

Some of Henry Stewart's friends thought it was high time for them to investigate. They crossed over to Hoy. O yes, said the Hoy wedding guests, they had got their invitations. After delivering them the bridegroom had gone shooting in the Trowieglen. Most likely he was spending a day in Rackwick, fishing for trout.

The searchers went through the dark valley into Rackwick.

O yes, the Rackwick folk said, Henry Stewart had been in Rackwick, but he had been very disappointed because the shooting had been poor...

Some of the young Rackwick men said that Suleskerry was the place to shoot birds. Henry should spend a few hours there. They were prepared to sail him there in a yawl.

They went, on a fine summer day, with a favourable wind, but they hadn't returned. And the Rackwick folk shook their heads, in growing fear and bewilderment. The weather was still good.

The searchers set sail for Suleskerry at once. There they found Henry Stewart and the young Rackwick men lying dead among the rocks. The sea birds had been at their faces and hands.

There was only one possible explanation. The hunters had leapt on to the rock without securing their boat. The boat had drifted off, with the guns on board. They had died of hunger and exposure...

Meantime, it had been decided to go on with the feast in the Waters' barn. The bridegroom was bound to arrive before the dancing and fiddling and ale drinking were over.

And in fact he did; but it was a bird-scarred corpse that Helen Waters took in her arms[1].

The story is one of the legends in the old *Orkney Book* (1909). The author was John Malcolm. I wonder to what extent it was based on actuality, or whether it is pure invention? The story bears all the marks of high romanticism; even to the extent of having an old gangrel witch called Annie Fae, whom I haven't mentioned at all...

I would welcome, for private reasons, some opinion as to the tale's authenticity.

1 This story was expanded into a fullscale story and published in *The Two Fiddlers* (Chatto and Windus) 1974.

The Battle of Summerdale

15.3.1973

Seeing that it was one of the first fine spring days. my friend Stan took me for a run in his car on Wednesday afternoon. We went round by Houton—every time an Orcadian views Houton nowadays he should esteem as a precious moment—and along the Germiston Road to Stenness, and home again. It was a day of mellow sunshine with a swathing of mist on the hills. One reason I wanted to go that way was to glimpse again the battlefield of Summerdale, where in 1529 there was a fierce, bloody brawl between the forces of the Scottish crown and the Orkney rebels. The Scottish army—mainly Caithnessians led by Lord William Sinclair—was mauled terribly by the stone-throwing, flail-swinging Orkneymen. It is said—though I think there must be some exaggeration here—that the Caithness soldiers were killed to the last man.

The problem about this skirmish—for battle is too grand a word for it—is: why did it come to he fought on the bleak Orphir-Stenness border, far from any possible military objective? You would think that Lord William and his loyal soldiers, having landed at Houton, would have marched at once on Kirkwall.

It so happened that the same evening I got a glimpse in a friend's house of John Gunn's book for boys, *The Fight at Summerdale*. John Gunn, though a worthy Orkneyman, is not one of my favourite writers of fiction. But it was interesting to read his explanation of the locale of the battle. Lord William (says Gunn) intended to land at Scapa and assault the rebel town of Kirkwall from there. His ships miscarried in a sudden fog and beached at Houton instead. He was informed there that Kirkwall was twelve miles distant along the shore road... After some fearful melodramatic bargainings with a witch— events that don't concern us here—the Caithness army marched for Kirkwall. When they came to the Loch of Kirbister they thought it was an arm of the sea and marched along the margin, keeping the water on their right (as the Orphir men had instructed them).

And there, among the hills, the fury of the Orkneymen burst upon them and obliterated them[1].

1 This story is also in *The Two Fiddlers*.

It is not an entirely satisfactory theory.

I am interested because I am writing a brief account of Summerdale for young readers: more impressionistic than historical. I think it likely that Lord William Sinclair marched the way he did because he knew that Orkneymen from all the parishes and districts were gathering there, among the hills; and he had to defeat that army before he turned his attention to the well-fortified town of Kirkwall.

The First Air Raid

22.3.1973

It was very interesting to read in last week's *Orcadian* John Pottinger's account of the German air raid of March 1940, in which the first British civilian casualty of the war occurred.

I remember the evening well.

The previous months, ever since 3rd September, had been marked by many phoney air raids. At school, the classes trooped into the sandbagged shelters, every child with his gas mask slung over his shoulder, at the banshee wailing of the sirens. And trooped back again, half an hour later, at the all-clear. (One can imagine what disruption our education suffered.)

Nothing happened. No bombs fell. No bombs would ever fall. Instead of being grateful we school children got increasingly bored with the war.

That Saturday in March was a fine day: with spring thrusting up everywhere through the drabness of war. It is always a season of unspoken happiness and expectation for young folk.

Early in the evening the siren began to wail and yodel. But it didn't bring the golfers in from the golf course and it didn't bring the shoppers back from the town. (The shops were open on Saturday evenings then; and my mother was away getting the weekend provisions.)

Suddenly the carnival started. We had never seen or heard anything like it. The housing scheme shook and stoddered with appalling din. I can't remember that anyone went to the air-raid shelter in the next field: there was too much excitement for thoughts of safety. Even at that age, anyhow, I remember thinking that I would rather die in the open air than in a black, crowded, claustrophobic shelter.

The flash of the anti-aircraft guns was the most exciting thing of all. The air above Scapa Flow was deluged with puffballs. The guns stabbed vividly against the dark backcloth of Hoy. The appalling din went on and on; and in the brief intervals we could hear the undulating drone of German bombers. The evening went on, with growing earthquakes and volcanoes.

Then, as suddenly as it had begun, the sounds of war ebbed; and after a while the all-clear went.

There was plenty to talk about that night round the supper table: and mainly a rumour, growing before long to a certainty, that the pastoral hamlet of Brig-o-Waithe had been 'strafed'.

We boys walked out to the place where the two waters meet, the next day (Sunday), and saw the craters and ruins, and handled the bomb fins. We felt then a first quickening of the blood—a wonderment and excitement touched with fear. The war was real, right enough, and it had come to us; and it might well come again, and closer.

Orkney Books

5.4.1973

Why did it suddenly become desirable to have a collection of Orkney books? It wasn't always so; though here and there a few islanders kept a tenacious hold on every Orkney item they could get their hands on. I remember the Orkney Enterprise Exhibition of 1948, when stacks of Orkney books were sold at the bookstall for very modest prices. (I got a copy of the *Report of the Orkney Crofters' Commission* for a shilling. I no longer have it—somebody must have borrowed it—can I please have it back?...)

I wish now I had bought fifty of them.

One afternoon towards the end of the war I was in Rendall's printing office in Stromness and they gave me, free, a copy of *Two Old Pulpit Worthies of Orkney* by Alexander Goodfellow. There was a stack of copies slowly mouldering in the rafters. Mr Goodfellow's book is not a peerless work of prose but I imagine you would have to pay at least £2 for a copy today.

Edinburgh used to be famous for its second-hand book shops. On George IV Bridge was Grant's open-air bookstall, and many an hour I passed there when I was a student... One morning, on my way to a literature lecture, what did I see in Grant's stall but two well-known Orkney books: *Footprints of the Creator, or, The Asterolepis of Stromness* by Hugh Miller, and *Rambles in the Far North* by Fergusson. I got them for a shilling each. I would not part with either, at today's prices, for a fiver.

And in 1947 I saw a first edition of Scott's *The Pirate* advertised in a second-hand bookseller's list, in three volumes, for seven-and-six. Needless to say I still have that valuable item (though I don't read it any more)... From that same bookseller in Wishaw, I got for six bob a peerless copy of *Records of the Earldom*, one of the most fascinating of all Orkney books. In 1965 I bought a brand-new copy of *The Orkney Norn* in Leonard's, Kirkwall, for £2. Both these books would cost a small fortune now.

I'm glad I'm not a collector of Orkney books, otherwise I would find the present situation very frustrating. I wish this mad gale of inflation would die down quickly. But as things are, I look over at the little bookcase that holds my few Orkney books, and I think complacently, 'There must be three hundred quid's worth in that lot...'

An Austere April

3.5.1973

There has never been an April like this for a long time, with cold northerly winds streaming over the islands day after day. It has not been really bad weather—it was always a pleasure to be out, even on the coldest day—but in April one expects a little sweetness and warmth.

On Thursday last it came—a peerless day—all blue sky and blue pellucid waters and a warmth on the flesh for the first time since September. I sat for more than an hour on the Stromness shore of Hoy Sound, on a warm rock, and watched the tide brimming in. A motor-boat struggled westwards like a fly caught in glue. First Angus Brown's boat, and then the *St Ola*, came swiftly up on the flood.

Gradually the tide encroached. Where a dry rock had stood twenty minutes before was all seething and dazzlement, and in another ten minutes it would be drowned. A bigger wave broke and fell, green and glittering, on either side of the flat rock I was sitting on. It was time to be going...

The good weather reached into Friday. It encouraged me to get my winter growth of hair shorn. In the afternoon I was pleased to see the new tennis court at Ness being utilised for the first time, by schoolgirls on 'outdoor activities'. (We never had fun like that in our schooldays.) And over the new bowling green thin jets of water were playing. It might be pleasant to take up bowls this summer.

I remember how delightful were the summer evenings, in the forties and fifties, on the putting green. (The Stromness course was mostly hills and valleys—one depended for success on luck or on absolute precision—the merest whisker of miscalculation sent your ball curving among the lupins...) Alas, that delightful putting green is no more: or, at least, they say a truncated version will come into being sometime. The new bowling green, an immaculate green table, has usurped most of its space. Perhaps, given the chance, the bowlers of Ness will enjoy the same magical summer evenings as the oldtime putters: Jimmy Bruce, Willie Rendall, Bill Robertson, Jimmy Harvey, Bill Spence, Rev J. Thomson.

First hints of summer everywhere, then, on Thursday and Friday of last week. Then late on Friday night a blizzard came hurtling out of the north, with snowflakes as big as florins. It was beautiful, in a way, that silver-dark drift against the street lamps; but this year April, with its 'girlish laughter, girlish tears', has been more of a cold austere maiden lady than a girl.

The Use of Poetry

10.5.1973

Nearly everybody who writes to me from the south mentions, somewhere in the letter, and in tones varying from apprehension to horror, the black wave about to break over Orkney—OIL. Our friends seem to be far more concerned than the Orkney folk themselves. Is it that we are longing for something of the excitement, and splurge of money, that two world wars brought to the islands? Or is there something serene and wise in the Orkney character that can see the timeless beyond the fret and filth of the moment—like Robert Rendall's crofter? I would like to think the second situation applied to us, but it seems that, in general, the average outlook is depressingly materialistic.

It is the possibility of environmental pollution that is most disturbing of all; hills torn to pieces, fish floating belly-up in the sea, stenches in the wind.

Whenever I feel too utterly depressed by the prospect in front of us, I am cheered by a line of the poet Gerard Manley Hopkins—'There lives the dearest freshness deep down things...' He lived at a time when industrialism was spreading its unutterable ugliness all over the pastoral hills and villages of England. What he is saying is: no matter how grievously men tear and rend and filthy nature, the essential roots and sources of life go very deep; so deep that they can never really be touched, and they will go on sending up new springs and new blossoms till the end. 'There lives the dearest freshness deep down things.'

It is a consolation of a kind—less so, perhaps, when one has come to love a place, and only three-score-and-ten years are allotted; and it may take many centuries for the pristine freshness to overcome the entrenched rust, and steel, and concrete.

A Burning

17.5.1973

They were to do two plays of mine called *Witch* and *The Return of the Women* at the Close Theatre in Glasgow last weekend. The post one afternoon brought two complimentary tickets (not that I could possibly travel so far, at such short notice). The next morning, sleepily, I turned on the bedside transistor, and the man on the Scottish News said that the Close Theatre and the Citizens' Theatre and a bingo hall next door had all gone up in flames.

However, the indomitable Strathclyde Theatre Group promptly moved into another theatre, Partick Newton Church.

At the end of June they will be bringing the plays to Orkney; which is only right, I suppose, since Orkney is the place where the plays originated.

I should put 'plays' in inverted commas, because *Witch* was written as a short story, and *The Return of the Women* was written as a kind of prose-poem for seven women's voices: a threnody not meant for the stage.

It should be interesting to see what they make of it.

* * *

I see that the signs bearing the names of closes have gone up— Christie's Lane, Leslie's Close, etc—all except Puffer's Close.

I wonder sometimes if these names should be fixed, in this way, for all time? Dare we impose our transitory nomenclature on future generations?

For obviously it was not always, for example, Christie's Lane. If that rocky ascent had a name at all, it was something different before the advent of Rev James Christie, at the century's turn, to the big Manse crowning the brae. And what was Leslie's Close before the Leslies lived there? We may be sure it was something different. We may be sure our grandchildren will have another name for it still.

Garrioch's Close, after all, was changed to Khyber Pass. And what was called Copland's Pier in my childhood was Ronaldson's Pier to an earlier generation.

I think, on the whole, I am in favour of leaving the situation fluid.
Let each new generation supply its own names. It will be interesting
to see what the final decision is between Lord Dundas and a man who
used to stand, day-long, against the wall of Angus Brown's house—
the town crier, who was called James Leask, alias the Puffer[1]—and
who did in fact live in that beautiful close that climbs up to Cliff
Cottage and the Braes.

An Angry Crofter

24.5.1973

The first tourists are beginning to filter in—the early tremors of a
tide that will pour through Orkney in July, August, September.

Now that we are committed to tourism as one of our major
industries, the tide can be expected to flood in higher and higher in
the summers to come.

What to think about it all puzzles the mind. I am one of those who
like to see new faces about the street. Last summer there were plenty
of visitors—many a day they seemed to outnumber the inhabitants of
Stromness. Young folk predominated, with beards and questing eyes
and rucksacks and outlandish clothes. (In the summers immediately
after the war—and certainly before the war—the impression I have of
a tourist is somebody elderly and sedate and middle class. All that has
changed.)

Last summer, it seemed to this unbiased observer, Orkney had about
as many tourists as it could take. Anything more, and the delicate
balance between locals and visitors would be upset. But that might
be a totally wrong impression. We will have to wait and see.

Modern Orkney folk are delighted to welcome strangers and visitors.

1 Some of the folk who lived there objected to the name 'Puffer's Close'—
  the Puffer was a man of sombre and powerful character who flourished a
  half-century ago.

But imagine a crofter on the outskirts of Stromness who had never seen 'fok f'ae aff' in his life, in the year 1810.

A reader in Edinburgh has kindly sent me a photostat of a few pages of a book called *Travels in Iceland*. On the way to Iceland the *Elbe*—that was the name of the ship—sheltered in the harbour of Stromness. The author and his companions spent an evening at the Manse, with Rev W. Clouston. 'Teetotalism being then unheard of, brandy, and some excellent cinnamon water manufactured by Mrs Clouston, were handed about before and after tea...'

The tourists then went for a stroll among the fields. 'It seems,' wrote the traveller, 'that the people of Orkney are ... exceedingly jealous of strangers...' For while they were sketching some cottages, 'an old man, who was busy in planting potatoes at a little distance, on seeing us thus employed, left his work and, walking up, with as much fierceness as his weather-beaten countenance could express, roughly demanded what we were doing, and why we dared to go into the houses to frighten the children...'

We are more gentle with our visitors nowadays.

The 7:84 Theatre Company

31.5.1973

A talented group of players came to Orkney last week, and were well-nigh ignored. I refer to the 7:84 players and their production of *The Cheviot, the Stag, and the Black, Black Oil*, in Stromness, Kirkwall and Orphir.

I suppose you could call it a play, but it is more of an 'entertainment', with song, dance, poetry, fiddle-music, farce, tragedy, and audience participation—a fascinating patchwork with one clear theme—the tragic history of the Highlands of Scotland since the Battle of Culloden, with emptying glens and a broken culture. Nor is the end yet, for the oilmen are poised to move in...

Surely that ought to mean something to all Orcadians. For we too had our clearances, and we are going to have oil, and the whole pattern of our life is going to be changed. Yet only about 27 folk turned up to see the play in Stromness; and (I'm told) about a score in Kirkwall. The Orphir folk responded best of all, perhaps because of the Houton involvement—that parish sent along a hundred or so to see a kind of play that has never been seen in Orkney before, and might well be a signpost to the kind of drama of the future.

Gone—fortunately—are the kailyard days in the Orkney theatre: when every realistic detail was crammed on to the stage, from the calendar on the wall to the rolling-pin on the dresser, and gales of mirth were evoked by the holding-up, for example, of a pair of outsize knickers, preferably with a large patch on them. In the 7:84 production the scenery was as sparse and evocative as Shakespeare's. And as for the message, it brought to a burning focus all the letters and debates and articles that have appeared in *The Orcadian* since the first rumours of oil began.

So, Orkney missed a unique opportunity last week to have its vision purified, in the great tradition, with laughter as well as with pity and sorrow. The immediate situation before Orkney would have been much clearer, in the communal mind, if a thousand or so folk had been compelled to go and see *The Cheviot, the Stag, and the Black, Black Oil* last week.

I can speak out frankly about this, for I share in the shame and the blame of non-attendance. That is to say, I did not go to the production in Stromness, not knowing what to expect (and also wishing to see *Cider with Rosie* on TV). The enthusiasm of my friends swept me along to Orphir two nights later, and I'm very glad I went.

Paperbacks

14.6.1973

A few days ago the publisher sent me six copies of a paperback called *An Orkney Tapestry*. It was my first 'opus' in paperback, and so it gave me particular pleasure.

Pleasure, yes—but where was the old thrill, the joy, the excitement? Once upon a time—so many years ago that I hate to think about it— there was no pleasure so acute as the handling of new books. When I say 'new books' I mean paperbacks, for of course to buy a newly published book was well out of my financial range. A new novel in 1939, by Eric Linklater or J. B. Priestley, cost seven-and-six—fancy that!

The pleasure of being able to buy books, and own them, and have a little private library, began in 1935, when 'Penguins' put out their first three titles: *Ariel*, by André Maurois, *A Farewell to Arms*, by Ernest Hemingway, and *Poet's Pub*, by Eric Linklater. Sixpence was the price; and even then I had to save up for a few weeks to be able to afford one.

But the enormous pleasure we all got from those early 'Penguins'! There's nothing like it at all now. I feel like Wordsworth watching the shepherd boy on a May morning—something has vanished from the earth... Rae's of Stromness got in stocks of the new Penguin Books as they were issued—two or three a month then, not the enormous variegated flood of the 1970s. My hands trembled as I took down from the shelf Neil Gunn's *Morning Tide*, or Maurice O'Sullivan's *Twenty Years A-Growing*, or E. M. Forster's *A Passage to India*—and handed over my sixpence and silently stole away. A book in those early days was the most exquisite pleasure that life could give.

It isn't that way any longer. To come on a book that one truly enjoys becomes a rarer and rarer experience. One reads, yes, and approves, and says, 'Oh good...' But the breathless excitement is no longer there.

And so, when I opened the little parcel the other day and saw my six copies of *An Orkney Tapestry* in paperback, all I could manage—while truly admiring the typography and the format—was a tepid 'Well, now, that's nice...'

Midsummer Day

28.6.1973

Midsummer in Orkney has lost its marvellous rituals, though the Rev Ewan Traill told me a few evenings ago that in Hoy, this year again, the fire is to be lit on the summit of the Ward Hill, and a service held afterwards at dawn in Rackwick.

But the thought that Orkney's vessel of light is full and overbrimming is always exciting. Thereafter—even though summer goes on ripening and mellowing through July and August—the darkness begins slowly to encroach.

I took the bus to Kirkwall on June 21: most of the travellers were tourists. When we left Stromness the sun was behind high drapes of fog. They shredded thin as the bus headed east, and Stenness and Firth lay lapped in sunlight. How beautiful the Orkney countryside is in June, with the grass lush and green, and the ditches full of wild flowers! Soon the curtains of fog swirled across the sun again, and Kirkwall was grey. (Why does the Stenness-Firth plain escape so much fog, I often wonder?)

St Magnus Cathedral, like the bus, was full of tourists. I had a pleasant talk for twenty minutes or so with the curator, Mr Albert Thomson. This building in the heart of Orkney we should be grateful for if only because to stroll through it for twenty minutes is like a long cool drink in the desert of time. Not every community is so fortunate.

Finally, in the late afternoon, the sun broke through the swathings. In the bus going home it was as hot as a greenhouse. Summer had arrived—in the opinion of most folk, not before time.

All this past week the evenings have been marvellous: the harbour a mirror brimming with luminous shadows. On Tuesday the sailing boats had hung becalmed on the water... The stillness, it seemed, might go on for ever. After midnight, when the sun of 1973 had exerted its utmost sway and majesty and still smouldered on under the northern sky, a diminished moon rose over Orphir and dipped its honey between the Holms and the plangent piers.

Phin

5.7.1973

We were driving through Finstown the other day, and one of the visitors in the car remarked on the beauty of its situation, and another wondered how it came by its name. (We had been discussing place names for a large part of the tour.)

It's a very curious story indeed.

Imagine an Irish soldier called Phin. He has fought (like thousands of his fellow countrymen) in most of the Peninsular battles, and more than likely he has been in the squares at Waterloo, and stood while the French artillery cut down swathes of men all round him, while all day long—time after time—the French cavalry surged up the ridge. And there he stands at sunset, still alive, and fed full with horrors, and exhausted, when the order comes to advance...

The problem is, once Napoleon is on St Helena, what to do with all these veterans, the tough hard humorous men who, for a shilling a week, have 'saved the sum of things'... Many, it seems, were sent away as far as possible from the big cities, where they might well become criminals, or agents of revolution. So, this Phin and a few hundred other veterans stepped one fine morning on to the shore of Stromness; and a few of them were detailed for such useless jobs as building walls on Brinkie's Brae. (Many of their descendants are still alive to this day in Stromness and the West Mainland.)

But Phin walked east and built himself a little hut in a lonely place above the Oyce at Firth; because the place reminded him of the small green hills of Ireland. Country folk began to call in at Phin's to hear his stories (for, like all his compatriots, he had a vivid and a charming tongue). And because the stories sounded better along with a mug of home-brew, Phin began to brew his own ale. As the ale was good too, the numbers who congregated at Phin's on a winter night grew and grew. And folk began to build houses in that pleasant valley, for Phin had (with a true soldier's eye) chosen his location well. What more fitting, when presently the hamlet was large enough to deserve a name, than to call it after the first inhabitant? And so it will be Finstown till the end of time...

'But surely,' one of the folk in the car said, 'Phin's ale house will have long since vanished.'

I may be wrong about this, but I seem to have heard somewhere that the present Pomona Inn stands on the site of Phin's original house.[1]

Quiet Places

19.7.1973

As I write this on the eve of Shopping Week, the flood of tourists is reaching the high level. No doubt scores of Glaswegians will step off the *St Ola* tomorrow, for the trades holiday in the west began today.

Stromness will be a multicoloured whirl all this week; there will be no getting away from the bands and the loudspeakers and the beer bottles. But on Monday peace comes flooding in, and then the tourist will be able to discover for himself the essential Stromness. (By the way, there seems to be no current Stromness guide book, and many a tourist is lost without that.)

Guide book or no, most tourists find their way sooner or later to the four-star places in Stromness—Brinkie's Brae, the Museum, Login's Well, the Lifeboat Station, the swimming pool, Warbeth beach, the Community Centre—and well worth a visit most of them are.

But I always think that the essential Stromness is to be found in quiet places that are apt to be overlooked. For example, there are those piers at the South End—Greig's and Flaws's—that haven't altered since Hamnavoe began to be built three hundred years ago... Khyber Pass is fine, and many a tourist sets foot there because the name intrigues him; but there are lovelier closes, e.g. the one that begins at the gents' hairdresser's and ascends via Cliff Cottage to the gate of the Braes (for a certain reason I will give it no name). That close too is a bit of very old Stromness... Warbeth beach is unsurpassed, but if you want to be by yourself for an enchanting hour or two drop down by a perilous

1 This was a piece of pure imagination. The true story of Phin and his troubles was published later. It is fascinating reading. *Phin of Finstown* by R. P. Fereday of Kirkwall. Printed by W. R. Rendall, Stromness: 1974.

footpath and enormous sloping rocks to one or other of the sheltered nooks under the cliff that Stromnessians call the Tender Tables. There are crannies there sheltered from almost any wind, and if the tide is flowing the rocks and seaweed and limpets slowly drown under a gleam and a sonority: sights and sounds that were there long before TV and motor cars... These are only a few out of a hundred enchanting places. In Shopping Week, I imagine, when all the revellers are at the Market Green or the Community Centre—it will be possible to slip away and relish their peace.

Stone Giants

26.7.1973

The tourists ask me, twenty times a summer at least, as the car goes past Brodgar, 'What were the stones put there for, anyway?' Nowadays nobody knows for sure.

But the Orcadians of three or four generations ago had no doubts at all. The standing stones that are everywhere in Orkney were giants. They did their business and held their revels by night. They were great stupid, blundering, fighting creatures. The sun was death to them, so they had heard, and therefore they didn't go about in the daytime.

What happened to the giants nobody knows for sure. But their last night on earth must have been spent in some kind of celebration. What is the Ring of Brodgar but the giants going round in a dance? The dancing had gone on since the previous sunset, and was scheduled to end half an hour before dawn. All the giants of Orkney were there. They drank hogshead after hogshead of heather ale, and the mirth waxed fast and furious round about midnight—it was like thunder rolling among the hills.

Whatever giantess it was who brewed the ale—probably Cubbie Roo[1] of Wyre's daughter—she had never made it stronger. Dance followed dance; the pipe music was like the howling of a tempest.

---

[1] A legendary giant whose name merged into a Viking chief, Kolbein Hruga of Wyre, by a mysterious alchemy of the folk-imagination.

Presently the soberest giant there said, 'It's a half-hour till sunrise,' and he lurched off home over the hills. Others left singly or in groups of two or three. Three lugged an inebriate one off in the direction of Maeshowe... 'Fools!' shouted Megalith the host. 'Cowards! Afraid of a blink of sunlight!' And he led the dancers who were left round in a rejoicing circle.

Then the sun rose and turned every giant in Orkney to stone—not only the dancers, but those who were speeding or staggering homewards. The tallest giant of them all was standing by the Loch of Stenness, thinking how delicious a drink of cold loch water would be after all that ale, when a sunbeam petrified him. The gods were merciful in the case of that giant—every New Year's morning they allow him to stoop down and take a sip of Loch Stenness.

Such is the story of the standing stones; but I don't suppose Professor Gordon Childe[1] would have entertained it for one moment.

Orkneyingar

2.8.1973

One of the most sought-after books in Orkney for several years past has been *The Orkneyinga Saga*. The last publication, Dr A. B. Taylor's translation, was from Oliver and Boyd in 1938, and it cost, I think, £1.25—a large sum in those pre-inflation days. Since then the *Saga*, arguably the most important book in Orkney literature, has got scarcer and scarcer. The lucky possessors of copies kept them jealously on their bookshelves, not to be loaned to a dear friend for even half a day. When copies did come up at sales they fetched huge prices. But still there was a hunger on the part of Orcadians to read the stormy and glorious record from all those hundreds of years ago. These were the kind of men our ancestors were. Familiar place names cropped up everywhere. In these present days of ghastly narrative styles, here was prose simple, direct, and dramatic.

1 Archaeologist—author of *Skara Brae*.

There were hopeful rumours that Dr Taylor was going to bring out a new edition of the *Saga*; if so, his death last year must have been a sad interruption to any plan of the kind.

We knew that Penguin Books had been putting out a series of saga translations, and hoped that Messrs Magnusson and Palsson might get round at last to *The Orkneyinga Saga*. But it seems that we might have to wait for a while[1].

In the midst of all that gloom, suddenly a piece of good news. Early on Monday morning last I was walking along the street when I saw a copy of *The Orkneyinga Saga* in an unfamiliar format in the window of Charles Senior's bookshop. It proved to be, when I enquired, a facsimile reproduction of the Anderson edition of the *Saga* of 1873. It is now put out by the Mercat Press, Edinburgh, price £4.50—a reasonable price considering the feverish state of money these days. I bought a copy, of course. It looks handsome in the bookcase. And it is fascinating to compare that translation with Taylor's and with Dasent's...

Dasent was a great translator. I was lucky enough to discover in Mr Senior's shop too a first edition in two volumes of Dasent's translation of the greatest of all sagas, *Burnt Njal*. They knew how to turn out books in those days, with magnificent bindings and printing that is a delight to the eye. That edition of *Burnt Njal* is among my greatest treasures.

Scraps of Paper

23.8.1973

There used to be a time—not so long ago either—when people who wrote for a living threw away all their rough jottings and early shapings, and even the fair copy that is produced with so much sweat and labour. Nothing mattered in the end but the finished article— the ordered print on the page, with its imaginings and rhapsodies or mere information.

1 Penguin published a translation by Hermann Palsson and Paul Edwards in 1981.

All that has changed of recent years. A writer throws away nothing—not the least fragment of a whim that he jots down on a matchbox in the middle of a street, when he should be concentrating on getting his messages and picking his way between tourists and traffic.

Today it seems there is a market for almost anything. Somebody somewhere wants old cocoa-tins or bottles or brush handles. Among other things they want the scrawls of writers, however fragmentary, messy and incomprehensible. Why? In order, possibly, that some student in the year 2000, avid for a PhD, might sieve through all those blots and scratchings in order to find out the way a certain person's mind worked in the nineteen-seventies. Well, good luck to the unborn scholars, and deepest sympathy. Whatever the reason, the little scraps of paper with a few words on them, and the scarred and gory rough work, and the neat immaculate fair copies—that I used to light the fire with in the mornings of yore—are now carefully labelled and put away in a drawer until the arrival of the manuscript dealer.

There is many a way to turn an honest shilling nowadays. Even this humble 'Letter from Hamnavoe' in MS will escape the flames, the lavatory bowl, and the dustbin.

Saga Drawings

30.8.1973

There's such a hunger for *The Orkneyinga Saga* nowadays that the five hundred numbered copies of the Anderson edition (1873)—recently published in Edinburgh—must be almost exhausted. Certainly Orkney's quota vanished like snow on a June day...

What is even more urgently needed is a translation in the modern idiom. Such swift exciting narrative, such masterly characterisation, all accomplished in a few strokes—it puts the vast majority of modern novels to shame.

One does not normally associate the *Saga* with illustrations—simply because it has never been illustrated—but the other evening I saw a score of drawings that Ian MacInnes had prepared for the edition that Dr A. B. Taylor intended to put out before his sad death last year.

They are masterly drawings, which catch perfectly the drama and the humour and the earthiness of the text. The artist of course knows his Orkney well, and so the background in every drawing is utterly authentic and exact.

There they are, all the great moments of the *Saga*—the forcible baptism of Earl Sigurd; Earl Hakon and the wizard: Earl Harald's poisoned shirt; the martyrdom in Egilsay; Sweyn Asleifson and Sweyn Breastrope; Earl Thorfinn and the King of Norway breaking bread together on shipboard... And, besides those great moments, there are beautiful drawings of the way of life of the common people.

I hope very much that in the near future we may have Dr Taylor's— or some other—modern translation, enriched with Ian MacInnes's marvellous illustrations.

A King in Sandwick

13.9.1973

I stumbled by chance on a curious piece of legend the other day. I wonder if any reader will be able to fill it out a little?

Four and a half centuries ago a stranger knocked at a farmhouse door in Sandwick and asked if there was any work for him to do. He looked a decent enough young man, though his hands were white as meal and delicate-looking; but the farmer took him in and gave him his dinner.

The courteous farm folk could see that the stranger didn't want to be questioned too closely as to who he was or where he had come from. They talked instead about the land and the crops and animals. The man seemed to be very interested in what they had to tell him.

He appeared to be even more interested in the daughter of the house when she appeared. It was obvious, too, from her smiles and blushes, that she didn't think poorly of him.

In the end the Sandwick farmer agreed to employ his guest. He was obviously unsuited for farm work, but he did his best and they didn't drive him too hard.

Indeed the daughter of the farm lavished much kindness on him, and she saw to it that he got the best of food the farm could offer, and a soft bed after his labours of the day.

No doubt that girl was a great consolation to her father's new farm servant.

He disappeared as suddenly and mysteriously as he had come but with new muscles on his shoulders and calluses on his hands: and some knowledge of what it was to be a farmer in the farthest reaches of the kingdom of Scotland in those days.

He had much need of such knowledge, for he was in fact King James the Fifth of Scotland, and all he got from his courtiers was flattery and vague assurances that all was well...

The king, it seemed, chose this disguise—and several others, like the clothes of baker, weaver, cobbler, miller—to discover how things truly were in those days with the people he ruled over.[1]

The Lammas Market

20.9.1973

I had quite forgotten that Tuesday, 4th September, was Stromness Market Day until I read a paragraph in *Stromness and Round About* on the subject. It serves to show how that once great day is now fixed like a fossil in history.

It used to be a great day, especially for children. It came just a week after school reassembled, and so it brought a last wild sweet taste of freedom.

---

1 This is the embryo of the story 'The King in Rags', from *The Two Fiddlers* (Chatto & Windus, 1974).

And then the 'fairings'. From this neighbour you might get a threepenny bit and from that other a sixpence. Besides which you had been saving up as best you could, all through August. One market day I had five shillings, and I felt as rich as Croesus. In the middle of the night, what with a surfeit of ice cream, liquorice, chocolate, pears, lemonade and more ice cream, I was as wretched as Nebuchadnezzar... But still, I wouldn't have missed that day for anything.

The first Tuesday of September was a day of hustle and excitement. The town was crowded, for one thing, mainly with folk from the parishes. How wonderful to be lost in that dense throng between the Post Office and the Pier Head, and then suddenly to emerge into the square of enchantment where the stalls were: the fruit and ice cream sellers, the cheapjack, the Indian silk merchants, the rifle booths, the roll-the-penny stall, Charlie Riccolo and his roulette wheel, the fortune tellers, the swing boats, the merry-go-round, the coconut shy, the goldfish stall! The cries of 'the marketmen' were pure poetry. And the litter everywhere about the pier head was stuff of paradise. You stood for ten minutes, ice cream cone in hand, looking at the broken-nosed, dressing-gowned boxers issuing challenges outside their huge booth; then distant enchanting cries drew you back into the heart of the festival once more. The day kept shifting like a wonderful kaleidoscope.

And then, at last, night, when the naphtha flares leapt and hissed about the booths—and the five shillings had dwindled to fivepence—and the body was soaked with luxury and excitement and fatigue!...

They don't make days like that nowadays.

An Amateur Guide

27.9.1973

How many times this year have I been at the Brough of Birsay and Skara Brae, and across the Barriers, and watched Eynhallow and Rousay from the Evie Road? It seems like a score of times—it seems I have been there every other day since the beginning of June.

The fact is, visitors to Orkney expect to be taken to see these places. They have read about them and heard about them, and pinpointed them on their maps. They have worked themselves into a great hunger, in anticipation. And they think they would be none the worse of having a local guide. So their car—for I have none—heads north. In the back seat repose a camera and binoculars, and possibly map, guidebook, bird book... Off we go.

And 'Oh,' they exclaim, gingerly walking along the clifftops of Yesnaby, 'Isn't this marvellous!' The element of danger puts an extra thrill in their voices. They watch the slow heave of the Atlantic against the crags, and how the rocks tease it into immaculate dazzling lace...

Then, after a half-hour of lyricism and exclamations (not on my part—I've been through it all before), on we go to Skaill. More raptures, more joy, more wonderment—at the sweep of the beach and the mill and the stone-age village and the 17th century house...

North from Skaill there is all the tedious business of telling them of Kitchener and his memorial, and differentiating carefully between the palace of the Stuart earls and the palace of the Norse earls, and putting in a word or two about Magnus, earl and saint... Every bit of information is received with reverence. (But my tongue is long since weary with telling it.)

More raptures over Eynhallow and its roosts, and Rousay. 'What is that island in the distance?' ... 'Westray,' I answer with a sigh. 'And there is Wyre, where Edwin Muir and Bjarni Kolbeinson, great poets, warmed their hands at the same hearthstone... ' 'And that over there is Egilsay, where Magnus weltered in blood and glory.'

Cameras click, binoculars range over the bird-fretted sky, for the hundredth time...

Replete—them with the delights of tourism, I with boredom—we have a pint at the Merkister before returning to the Venice of the North.

Don't get me wrong, dear readers—I would not change these landscapes for all the languors of the Bahamas and all the antiquities of Egypt.

A Minor Macbeth

Looking through the sitting-room window, I can see a segment of harbour, and further off, between the Outer Holm and Clestrain shore, a thin gleam of sea. It suddenly struck me this afternoon that that piece of sea was where Gow the pirate cast anchor on a winter day in 1725.

Whatever possessed the man to do such a risky thing?

They say the net was closing in on him—his wild winter of murder and piracy was the hottest news in the Mediterranean and the North Atlantic—the Admiralty was plotting his course remorselessly from outrage to outrage. Some day soon they would forestall him and that would be the end of that ship of cut-throats...

So Gow slipped quietly into the Cairston roads; and decided to lie low for a while, maybe till the winter was over, maybe for ever.

He was taking an enormous risk. He was a Stromness man, well known to everyone. That—except for the fact that Admiralty intelligence might already (for all he knew) have been delivered to the gentry of Orkney—he could handle with ease, for he had natural charm and intelligence. But how did he ever think he could keep that crew of savages in order all through the darkness, the storms, the low rations of an Orkney winter?

Indeed his crew in the end was his undoing. They soon tore off their civil masks, and began to thieve and fight in every doorway of Hamnavoe. Then the fat was in the fire for Gow.

There may have been a more subtle reason that took Gow to his homeland. He was not a ferocious beast like some of his subordinates—Winter and Rollson and MacAulay. I think of him rather as a kind of minor Macbeth, sickened at last by the welter of murder and loot he had initiated. There is reason to think that he was touched by the presence on board of a ten-year-old Swedish boy, Peter Hanson.

Somewhere, then, between Labrador and Iceland, he experienced a kind of conversion. If he could only get back to the place where he had known innocence in all its fullness and purity, then perhaps that hideous year of piracy might be struck from his soul, and he could make a new beginning.

So one morning the folk of Stromness—Alexander Graham, a small boy, and Bessie Millie, a girl, among all the others—woke up to see this strange ship anchored beyond the Holms. And after a time a small boat rowed in to the piers, and a well-known handsome face smiled up at them. 'John Gow' went wonderingly from mouth to mouth. How well William Gow's boy had done in the seaports of Europe—here he was, master of a fine brig! Then they looked again and saw the dark, twisted faces and the smiles like rats at bow and stern.

Somehow the pieces did not fit.

The only thing that did fit was the hangman's rope at Wapping, London, seven months later; and Gow, because the rope was frayed in his case, had to endure the horror of a double hanging.

Hallowe'en

1.11.1973

The old wooden tub was taken out of the shed and set squarely on the flagstone floor. It was threequarters filled with water; maybe a kettleful of hot water was added to take the chill off. Then a poke bursting with apples was emptied into the tub, where they tossed and eddied and collided with each other—ruddy fragrant spheres.

One after another the young folk of the house, and their friends, had a go at seizing an apple between the teeth and so winning it for himself. It was no easy matter; the apple kept bobbing away from the closing mouth. At last, after several vain attempts, the technique was perfected—you manoeuvred the chosen apple towards the side of the tub with your head, and there it was cornered and transfixed and brought up into the lamplight. What laughter and applause then, round the saturated head! A towel was brought—the apple was munched to the core. Meantime the next celebrant in the rite of Hallowe'en was kneeling over the tub, choosing the biggest and ruddiest apple for the kill...

So it went on, until the last apple was brought out.

I have only a vague memory of what we did with the nuts—whether they were 'dooked' for too, or simply shared out—walnuts, hazelnuts, chestnuts, thinly scattered among a huge profusion of monkey nuts.

There were one or two variations; as when an apple coated with syrup was suspended from a rafter and the object of the exercise was to take a bite out of it. It was not so easy either, and meantime, cheeks and foreheads got stickier and stickier...

There must certainly be some reason rooted in old magic for these rituals. Of course the apples and the nuts marked the consummation of the fruitful year. Ahead stretched the gauntness and snows of winter.

I can't remember that we were ever scared by stories of the witches that were supposed to be particularly active on that night of all nights.

We munched the apples and cracked the nuts and dried our heads at the fire. Then it was bedtime.

Do Orcadians still go through these performances on Hallowe'en, I wonder? It was much more innocent fun than pulling gates off hinges and spraying walls with paint.

It was a season thick with excitement. A few nights later, and turnips were sculpted and daubed for Guy Fawkes.

A Boy's Week

8.11.1973

It's Friday afternoon—and why is it that Friday always has such a fragrance about it? Undoubtedly it goes back to schooldays, when Friday marked the end of that long week of reading and sums and geography. Friday after tea was the most magical time of the week— better even than Saturday with its boundless freedom.

On Friday evening you put on your Life Boy uniform—blue jersey, blue stockings with white hoops, sailor cap—and sallied with a carefree heart up the Kirk Road to the church hall for fretwork, netball, etc.

Every day had a flavour of its own. Monday was a drab affair. Not only did you have to creep like a snail unwillingly to school, but Monday was washing day all over Stromness. The washing of clothes was a much more strenuous duty in those days before automatic machines—it took up the whole day from morning to night, and the house was a clutter of washingboard, mangle, dampness, steam, bleach and soapflakes and blue. The only good thing about Monday was that you got ham-and-egg for dinner.

Tuesday was one of those nondescript days—it was dull and without personality. The only good thing was that *The Wizard* arrived by the *St Ola*.

Wednesday tasted of the earth. On that day the farmers and their wives came to Stromness on bike and cart, and there were horses on the street. Men from the parishes stood at the Pier Head and smoked their pipes and exchanged a few careful remarks about 'kye' and 'swine'.

Thursday had some light and leavening to it. You began to see light at the end of the tunnel. There was always the marvellous treat on Thursday evening, if you had been prudent enough to save up fourpence—the 'pictures' in the Town Hall, with Tom Mix and Felix the Cat.

The delights of Friday have been discussed.

Saturday is more difficult to give a taste of. Football, fishing, fighting, the spending of the Saturday penny, eating warm weekend pancakes—there was perhaps too much freedom, too much anarchy—the day is one grey happy confusion in the memory.

Of Sunday, all I can say about it is that it was unction and alabaster.

The Giving of Names

15.11.1973

'Gray's Noust' sounds all right on the tongue and in the ear. All credit to the Town Council—they have combined in this name for the new housing scheme beside the lifeboat station both the old inn and the boat shelter.

The giving of names is always a delicate and dicey business. When, some two years ago, five townsmen met together and decided, after a very brief discussion, to call a certain envisaged thoroughfare 'Ferry Road', the name was received with little warmth, and in some quarters with incredulity and ridicule. But the name is simple and descriptive, which is what a name should be nowadays. (I speak of course as an interested party.)

What I don't particularly like is the giving of a fancy name like 'Faravel' to a housing scheme. It is too overtly flowery. It has no real meaning at all. And yet the name has caught on—these houses will be Faravel till they are empty shells.

'Hoymansquoy' is a very felicitous name, with a lot of strength in it and a bit of mystery too. Who was the Hoyman who owned that piece of land? We will never know. But the name abides, and it is one of the finest names in the town.

It is true, of course, that names are bestowed nowadays out of mere whim and fancy, on people and houses and boats. But in olden times it was a matter of the deepest importance what name a child, for example, was called. For the name was supposed to influence his entire character—it set an inviolable seal on his life—it was his heraldic motto, something he had to live up to.

All that mystery has vanished from name-giving now, whether we like it or not. I think the best we can do nowadays is to be simple and straightforward when we consider giving a house or a district a name. That's why I think 'Ferry Road' is all right. If we can unite simplicity with history and a certain degree of euphony—as in 'Gray's Noust'— that is even better.

It is an area where it is possible to be sentimental, and even dead inaccurate—as can be verified from the names of scores of private houses in Orkney. The Norsemen knew better. They were plain and direct. When they called a house 'Hammar' it was because there was an outcrop of rock nearby; or 'Breck' or 'Lea', it was because these places were built on a slope—though how the 'Lea' slope differed exactly from the 'Breck' slope is a more difficult thing to answer.

The Hijacking of John Renton, Sailor

22.11.1973

A young man with a sailor's box on his shoulder knocks at a lodging house door in San Francisco. The sailor is nineteen years old, the year is 1867.

The landlord who opens the door has some difficulty in understanding what the sailor wants, perhaps because he speaks in a rare accent. The words are softly uttered, they go up and down, the sentence ends on a fairly high note (as if a question was being asked). In other words, the young sailor is an Orcadian. At last the landlord makes out that he wants a room for one night—that he is a sailor—that he has just arrived from Hong Kong on a windjammer—that he is about to join a steam vessel, the *Pacific*, carrying mail between Sydney and San Francisco.

The young man is taken in. He is shown an empty bunk upstairs where he can spend the night. He puts down his sea-chest beside it. The landlord is all smiles and affability.

Down below there is a bar, much frequented by sailors, also run by the landlord. He invites the sailor, once he has had a stroll around and seen some of the sights of San Francisco, to come in and have a drink at his expense.

As soon as John Renton—that is the sailor's name—is out of sight, the landlord loses his merry dimples and his flashings of teeth. He becomes very secret and conspiratorial, especially with one sleazy-looking customer. They whisper together. They point here and there—at the street outside, at the room above, at the harbour, at the bottles on the shelf. They are engaged on an immensely important piece of business, those two. The patrons have to bang their pewter mugs on the counter before they get service.

Whatever the nature of the business, at last an agreement is reached. The landlord and the sinister one shake hands. Then once more the landlord is all joviality and teeth-flashing. The customers get jugs of ale with bonnets of froth on them as soon as asked for.

John Renton enters the smoky bar just before closing time. He is given a hearty welcome and a glass of rum on the house. One by one the patrons drift out into the night, most of them down to the ships. The young Orkney sailor stays at the counter, sipping rum. At last he and the landlord are alone. 'You're good and welcome,' says the landlord, 'It's the best rum I got. It'll make you sleep good.'

John Renton drinks to the last drop.

He woke up, with leaden veins and a head that felt as if it had been cloven, on board the sailing ship *Reynard* of Boston, somewhere in mid-Pacific a few days later.

That was only the first extraordinary thing, apart from being born, that happened to John Renton in the brief thirty years of his life. I read it with interest the other day in Provost J. G. Marwick's *The Adventures of John Renton* (1935), now out of print. I thought, reading it, that it is a wonder Stromnessians don't show more interest in their fellow-townsman who lived for years among the Malaitans in the Pacific, and was finally murdered as an Australian government agent, at the age of thirty.

The Hoy Trust

29.11.1973

It's wonderful that something is going to be done at last for Hoy. Mr Stewart's[1] foresight and generosity will be remembered among the truly altruistic deeds that happen from time to time in the north.

It is when a community in a certain place is threatened with extinction that we come, often too late, to have a reverence and regard for the place and the kind of life that went on there.

The once-teeming life of Rackwick, for example, is now down to one inhabitant, Jack Rendall of Glen Farm. Orkney folk over the past dozen years or so have been saddened by the rapid depopulation of the place and have done their best to arrest the decay by restoring old, half-ruined crofts and living in them whenever they got the chance— an occasional weekend, perhaps, or a couple of weeks in the summer.

1 The laird of Hoy.

A holiday in Rackwick—only a few miles from home—has a fascination that Blackpool and Bournemouth could never rival. Even the frequent rain, in retrospect, falls joyously through the memory.

But holiday cottages, welcome though they are as attempts to keep the breath in a dying place, are no substitute for a community rooted and taking its bread from the soil. We wish the new Hoy Trust all success in its attempt to revitalise the most beautiful of the Orkneys.

To return again to Rackwick in particular: I wish something could be done to salvage all that is known about the valley, its crofts and its people. A year or two back, the Stromness Academy magazine had an excellent feature about the past of Rackwick. I remember about twenty years ago reading a manuscript book written by the late Mr Bremner, then Kirkwall harbourmaster, and himself a native of Rackwick. It was called *Hoy's Dark Romantic Isle* and contained a great wealth of remarkable material, especially about Rackwick. That manuscript must be lying in some desk somewhere. It's high time it was published.

And perhaps Jack Rendall could be persuaded to spend part of a winter jotting down some of his memories of the valley?

St Andrew's Day

6.12.1973

Today, as I write, is St Andrew's Day, November 30. I flipped through the *Radio Times* this morning to see if there would be anything in celebration of the day, but couldn't discover anything (unless *Blue Peter* on TV—Valerie Singleton in Edinburgh—might be a St Andrew's celebration of a sort: if it is, it doesn't specifically say so)... And on radio, as far as I can see, nothing at all.

It's too bad. I remember not so long ago that St Andrew's Day was celebrated over the air with Scottish music and poetry, and most years it made memorable listening—rich dark winter fare.

It's the same, recently, with Burns' Day (January 25). When I was a boy the wireless thrummed all evening with 'Tam O'Shanter',

'To a Mouse', 'Bonny Mary o' Argyle', 'Ae Fond Kiss', 'O Whistle and I'll Come to You My Lad'... And it was marvellous, sitting close to the old battery set and letting all that magic pour over you. Besides the song and poetry, there were generally—if I remember aright—one or two intelligent talks about Burns, and maybe on Children's Hour a wee play to take the tears to your eyes. (Burns and Mary Campbell, for example; or Burns and his brother Gilbert following the great ploughhorses on Mauchline Farm: and 'Hoch!' cries Gilbert, 'look at that, Rab—a wee bit moose runnan frae the ploo!...')

No more. Can it be that Burns is not the power he was in Scotland? If so, Lord help us all, for Burns with his great reserves of charity and joy has much to say to a pallid money-crazed society...

Hogmanay, of course, still gets a plug on the media—a feast of swirling kilts, Scotch 'coamics' at their awfullest and songs shot through and through with the awful brand of sentimentality that Scotland (alas!) specialises in.

Burns, John Barleycorn—we can recognise them when their names come up. But St Andrew, whose day this is: how does he come to be connected with Scotland? He probably didn't know that such a place as Scotland existed. And yet this unlettered Jewish fisherman has us in his care and keeping—having been blinded one day, suddenly, by a charity towards all men everywhere.

Winter at Maeshowe

20.12.1973

I suppose it only happens once in a decade—a clear south-west horizon on the afternoon of the winter solstice. One of the astonishing stories they used to tell about Maeshowe was that at sunset on the winter solstice, the sun for the only time shone through the long, low corridor and touched with light, fleetingly, the far wall of that chamber of death.

Could it really be that those primitive folk had such skill in building and engineering and astronomy that they could make this happen—

that they could so arrange their web of stone that the sun was made to shine where it had never managed to find a way all the rest of that bright year—here, now, in the very heart of darkness?

On the winter solstice of 1972 there fell such a day—a blue cloudless sky, and what in the circumstances is more important, no clouds on the horizon to cover up the setting sun.

Early in the afternoon we set out for Stenness. We weren't the only folk to seize the opportunity—other cars were parked at Tormiston, and we could see a group of figures round the chamber opening.

Everything worked out. The sun made a cloudless descent. The interior of the chamber was full of crepuscular whispering figures. Then the sunset flowered on the stone—the last beam of light of the shortest day—and it glowed briefly on a wall that at every other time of the year is dark.

What did these old Orcadians mean by it? Why did they go to so much trouble?... We can guess, and perhaps with some confidence, that they wanted to celebrate the balance of light and darkness, summer and winter, life and death. At the time of the year's deepest darkness, a finger of light touches the chamber of death; there is a hint of a promise of resurrection.

The first Stenness men were good mystics as well as good builders, astronomers and hunters.

The Bishop's Palace, Kirkwall

17.1.1974

A friend of mine in Perthshire sent me a beautiful Christmas gift—a coloured Daniell print of the Bishop's Palace. In the spring of 1973 he had presented me with the Earl's Palace in the same series: so this is a companion piece.

Not knowing much about art or engraving, I have no idea of the artistic merit of a Daniell print. What they do evoke is the romantic atmosphere of the time—the date on them is 1821, the year that Keats and Shelley and Byron were the guttering remnants of magnificent fires. It was the year, too, I think, that *The Pirate* was published. The same bouquet rises from the prints and the prose—rather consciously melancholy, mysterious, aloof.

Apparently, Daniell the artist—or were there two of them, brothers?—went all round Scotland recording the various regions. It must have seemed a novel and splendid idea at the time, for hitherto nobody had bothered. (Up to that period such natural phenomena as mountains, waves, rocks had seemed to educated people to be bits of primeval savagery, to be avoided if at all possible. The only things worth recording were towns and landscape gardens, where man's fine artistry was to be admired, and the postures of antique heroes, and copying from great renaissance masterpieces.)

But the Daniells expressed the new age. Potent mysterious spirits inhabited the rocks and the seas, and had a powerful and beneficent influence on men if only they opened their hearts to them. So, therefore, part of the job of artist and poet was to build bridges between man and nature. That, I think, is what the Daniells, and hundreds of other artists about their time, were trying to do... It was more than simply making a record of a place, the way photographers return now from their holidays with hundreds of coloured snapshots.

Marvellous as modern photography is, it doesn't have the same power as these old engravings to evoke the spirit of a place and an age.

As awe-inspiring as nature to the artist was 'the dark backward and abysm of time'...

There are figures in this print—women carrying yokes of water—but the building is the only true living thing. It broods in its decay on lost splendours, and on the greatest drama that ever took place within its walls—the death of the great King Hakon of Norway, in 1263, after the battle at Largs.

Orkney in World Literature

24.1.1974

Tomorrow is Burns' Day, when Orcadians feel more Scottish than at any other time of the year, except perhaps at the Scotland v England football international.

It may be that the time of year when a person is born influences his whole life. At any rate I think of Burns as a winter poet, not in the sense of coldness and sterility, but of the joyousness of winter (including whisky, ghosts, fiddling and dancing and singing, secret kisses under the stars, and warmth and goodfellowship round the fire).

A sad disappointment to us Orkney lovers of Burns is that he never once mentioned Orkney in his works. Could it be that he had never heard of our islands? Nonsense. If he wasn't exactly a scholar, he was a man of far-ranging intelligence. And that I think is another point against the theory that the Burns family of Kincardine and Ayrshire originated in some Burness district of Orkney. For if it had, the tradition was almost certain to have lingered in the family memory; and, as we know, the boy Burns was an avid listener to old wives' tales...

And so Orkney doesn't figure in any Burns index.

But then neither does it in the works of Shakespeare, Dante, Tolstoy, or Walt Whitman.

In Ernest Marwick's *An Anthology of Orkney Verse* there is a fascinating section called Travellers' Tales, consisting of poems in which Orkney is mentioned, ranging from the Latin poet Claudian (c 400AD) through the scurrility of J. Emerson, and Byron's horrible error when he described George Stewart of the *Bounty* as being 'the fair-hair'd offspring of the Hebrides', to a delightful narrative poem by the Poet Laureate John Masefield... The notorious 'Bloody Orkney' is not included. I have always thought that an overrated piece of satire; though life in wartime Yesnaby or Lyness must have been pretty awful for some city-bred soldiers.

The most delightful mention of Orkney in literature occurs in 'The Nun's Lament for Philip Sparrow', a fifteenth-century English poem by John Skelton. Philip was the nun's pet bird, until a cat put an end to it. Whereupon the nun proceeded to put on that cat a most uncharitable curse, till all the world, 'From ocean, the great sea, Unto the Isles of Orchadye' might wonder at the vengeance that has been taken on it... That little nun, at any rate, five hundred years ago, had heard of our islands.

A Crisis and an Election

21.2.1974

That was one of the best things to come out of the crisis, when they decided to close down TV at 10.30pm. A howl of rage went up from Muckle Flugga to the Lizard—what on earth would they do wanting their late-night telly? And couldn't the authorities stop it during the day for a while instead, so they could get lulled to sleep by their nightly anodyne—the benediction of that old one-eye in the corner of the living room.

So firmly, in a matter of twelve years or so, has the drug taken possession of us—and much of it (though not all) a dance of irrelevant shadows.

What a blessed relief it has been of late when 10.30 came, and you yanked the plug out of the wall. You could read, or write a letter, or converse with your friends for the last sweetest hour of the day—or simply drink your ale and dream.

But along comes this election. So important do politicians think themselves, apparently, that the economics of crisis are immediately jettisoned. Now half the night we have to watch the three superstars, and their satraps, posturing and mouthing. Deluge upon deluge of promise, argument, dire prophecy—and not only out of old one-eye, but from the radio too. As soon as I switch on the transistor in the morning, half-asleep, the politicians are at it again. And to think we will have to put up with the rant for twelve more days!

* * *

I didn't know till a friend sent me a copy of the memorial service that Douglas Young was dead.

He was in the vanguard of the Scottish 'literary renaissance' and wrote some of the best lyrics in Lallans of the nineteen-forties. He was more than a poet—he had the courage to go to prison for his convictions during the war. And he was a brilliant classical scholar.

I met him only once, and briefly, at the unveiling of the plaque to Edwin Muir in St Magnus a few years back. He gave the moving oration.

During the memorial service in the University Chapel, St Andrews (his alma mater), his peerless Lallans translation of the 23rd Psalm was read:

> The Lord's my herd, I sall nocht want,
>   Whaur green the gresses grow
> Sall be my fauld. He caas me aye
>   Whaur fresh sweet burnies rowe.

Elections

28.2.1974

This is the day. Before midnight we will know who is to govern us for the next five years. Good luck to them, whoever they are—they're going to need it.

It seems there are not nearly so many people turning up at local halls to hear the candidates as there used to be. There, again, it's the TV to blame. Who's going to leave the fireside on a winter night to sit in a cold hall? None but the faithful.

Before television, election meetings were enormously popular. It was not only public-spiritedness that lured Stromnessians in their hundreds to the Town Hall—it was in the hope of hearing some spirited heckling, and mingled wit and fury and fun.

The first Orkney MP whom ever I cast eyes on, as a small boy, was Sir Robert Hamilton. There he walked along the street and up to the Town Hall, a grave, bearded figure. I thought he looked very like King George the Fifth. He seemed to be from everlasting to everlasting.

Came the 1935 election. As boys—somewhat older now—we weren't allowed to the meetings. But we climbed walls and railings and glimpsed Sir Robert gesturing on the platform, and Mr James Corrigall sitting at the table in support.

Stromness was supposed to be a radical town in those days. My father took the *Daily Herald* (a Labour paper) but still he supported Sir Robert Hamilton in the absence of a candidate further to the Left. Sir Robert still, in 1935, seemed indestructible. What a shock went through Stromness, therefore, when at the count Sir Robert was out to Major Neven-Spence by over two thousand votes!

That was the last Election for ten years. The next one, in July 1945, was by far the most exciting of all. The war was over. There was a Labour candidate for the first time, Prophet Smith. The Liberals put up a young, gifted, handsome candidate in Jo Grimond. Neven-Spence was still there, defending his unexpected gain of 1935.

No one knew exactly how—in these new circumstances—the pattern would arrange itself. The candidates' meetings in the town hall drew great crowds. There was considerable discussion, a constant seethe of excitement. We had to wait for weeks after polling day for the boxes to be opened—and there—in the midst of a Labour landslide nationwide—it showed Neven-Spence, Grimond, Smith in that order; but with only a few hundred votes separating them... It was very exciting indeed.

Eric Linklater at 75

7.3.1974

Eric Linklater is 75 this month, and his fellow-authors and friends are to honour him with a dinner at the New Club, Edinburgh, on 15th March.

Eric Linklater is one of Scotland's best storytellers ever. What Orcadian now in his forties or early fifties can ever forget his first reading of those early Linklaters—*Whitemaa's Saga*, *Magnus Merriman*, *Poet's Pub*? For many of us these books made living in Orkney an exciting and rich thing. I think it is in large measure owing to Eric Linklater that young Orcadians in the second quarter of this century came to love their islands so deeply. Before we got to know the *Saga* we had read *The Men of Ness*, and so, when the time came, we were prepared for the great stories of the Orkney Earls in Taylor's translation.

Besides being a novelist, Eric Linklater is a masterly short-story writer. 'Kind Kitty' is one of the most brilliant and hilarious short stories in the language. 'The Three Poets', and the tale of the picnic party that disappeared on Eynhallow, are not far behind. I often wish that he had spent more time on the short story—he is such a consummate master... In addition, he has written successful plays, biographies and autobiographies; and verse of great verve and wit.

So we salute this Orkney writer who has in our own day told stories with all the style and gusto of the old sagamen and who has also added what they lacked, a marvellous lyricism, a delight in the land and the shifting seas and skies of the north.

Miners

14.3.1974

So, the miners are going back to work on Monday. Those of us who have been saving candle-ends and storing bits of driftwood in their sheds, against the day of industrial Armageddon, can breathe easily again—at least for a time.

And yet, though they've caused us flutters of panic more than once in recent years, at the thought that our civilisation might gutter out in darkness and cold, there's hardly a person I speak to but has deep sympathy and admiration for the miners.

Who among us would spend his working week toiling in the black veins of the earth? Society in the past has not rewarded the miners adequately, to put it mildly. Yet, in spite of everything, the mining communities of Scotland—the only ones I know—remain the most cheerful and generous of people.

If any folk deserve to be well paid, it's them.

Stromness had miners too, a long time ago, though it's difficult to imagine anything about them or their work.

At the far end of Warbeth beach there is a craggy depression set flush in the greensward. Today it is hardly more than a scar, but in the 1930s the 'Miners' Hole' was aptly so called. Brave boys—not I— could crawl in quite a distance. Our fathers had a tale that the mine extended so far that at the distant face the tongs could be heard rattling in the hearth of Clook farm!

Apparently it was lead that those eighteenth-century miners were after. The Industrial Revolution was hungry for metals of every kind—the furthermost parts of the kingdom were rifled for their hidden riches. I must have read somewhere that lead-bearing ore was dug from the face of the Kame of Hoy even.

There is certainly lead at Warbeth. The boulders on the foreshore are heavy with ore. But in the end, probably for reasons of expense, the mine was never exploited to the full... After a year or two the Stromness lead miners, breathing sighs of relief, went back to their boats and crofts.

The Tides of Spring

21.3.1974

Today is the vernal equinox, one of the four magical times of the year. In the everlasting struggle between light and darkness both forces are locked together and motionless, on this day. From now on the darkness begins to give way.

I'm sure, if we could read the standing stones with true insight—the circles and the solitary ones—some pattern would emerge at this time of year. But perhaps too many stones have disappeared over the centuries. Certainly modern man is not so sensitive to the subtleties of the seasons. The delights of March meant more to an old Orkney crofter than they do to an oilman.

And yet March was a hard time of year in the north. 'As the day lengthens the caald strengthens,' the old folk said. This was the season they called 'the lang reed', when meal was low in the girnal, and the dried cuithes and smoked mutton were wearing done. Often the old Orkneymen must have been hungry in the last days of March.

But the new light put heart into them. The first flowers were breaking out of the earth. There were white tremulous lambs on the hills. The seed was in the earth. The heather fires answered each other from hill to hill.

Perhaps, at the very end of March, there might be snowflakes in the wind, to remind the crofter that winter, though he was slowly yielding, had dark strength in him still.

But by April the tides of light and growth were flooding everywhere. All that was required (apart from hard work, and that was perennial, the yoke of Adam) were patience and faith; in due time would come the bringing in of the sheaves and the Harvest Home.

We have lost this relish for the eternal drama of light and darkness, to a great extent. Civilisation has ruined the natural rhythms. But not, I think, entirely. We would not be human if we did not experience a lightening of the spirits at this time of year. It never fails to work. Some day in late March or early April every old man, however weary of the struggle, feels fleetingly that he is a boy again; and that life, in spite of all, has been worth living.

Swans

28.3.1974

Last week, round about the equinox, there were three or four days of marvellous weather. People forgot about the sour winter just past, and turned smiling faces summerwards.

One afternoon when I took a seat at the Pier Head, what was brought out from the Eventide Club but a table and chairs and a set of dominoes, and the game was played for an hour and more in full sunlight—a thing that's never happened before at the height of summer...!

'This fine weather can't go on,' I said to myself in true Orkney style. But the next morning was, if anything, more beautiful. So I put away paper and pen and crossed the street to a small pier, and sat down on a concrete block near the edge. A young student hailed me from a flattie. He had been taking photographs all along the seafront. He beached the flattie and we chatted about old-time Stromness for half an hour or so. (It's hard to be precise, time had such a sweet flow in the spring sunshine.) Then he had to go home for his dinner.

It was ebbing fast. One of the two swans that have of recent years claimed this particular part of the harbour for their territory dipped immaculately into sight, as if it was expecting some tryst; and sure enough a woman from a nearby house came out with a bowl of scraps and flung them, piece by piece, to the huge white bird. It accepted them delicately, yet with a touch of arrogance, and the swirl of gulls that had arrived to share in the feast kept their distance. Having finished his meal, the swan departed in search of his mate (who must go, it seems, to another pier for her lunch). The gulls moved in then on the remnants of the feast.

These swans have been lending their pure white beauty to our piers at the South End for the past few years.

The tide ebbed rapidly. Soon the pier was standing with its stone feet in the ebb. The benign March sun continued to shine. I could have sat there all afternoon, but there was work to do, and I had a faint anguish of hunger inside me. That old Scottish conscience—'If you don't work you don't deserve to eat'—drew me indoors to my duties.

The Betting Men

4.4.1974

'The People of Orkney,' wrote Rev James Wallace nearly three hundred years ago, 'are much given to strong drink; the nature of the climate requires this'... I am quoting from memory. It is true that all over the northern hemisphere the people drink more of 'ardent liquors' than those who dwell in gentler sunnier latitudes. It is just a fact of nature—no praise or blame attaches.

But whatever else the Orcadians are given to, serious betting can't be charged against them.

When first I stayed in the south for a length of time, one of the strangest observable phenomena in public bars, about the middle part of the day, was the little furtive man who went here and there collecting slips of paper and silver coins. What on earth could that be? I was told that the 'bookies' runners' were on the job, collecting bets for their invisible masters. Later in the afternoon, after the race had been run in Liverpool or Ayr, back came the same little man with the winnings; but of course fortune had smiled on perhaps only one out of twenty.

Nothing daunted, the betting men furrowed their brows over the *Noon Record* or the racing section of the *Daily Express* once more. Hope springs eternal in the human breast, and each and every one of them was convinced that, later that same afternoon, a windfall would be theirs...

I was impressed by the tenacity of those punters. They were hooked on betting, only in a very mild way—being working men most of them, extravagant bets were beyond them. The rather strange thing is that then or now, I have never had the faintest itch in that direction. I much preferred to spend two bob on a sure, certain, delectable pint of Guinness.

When I told my Edinburgh friends that betting didn't enter into the Orcadians' scheme of things, they replied, 'Ah, but then there are no racecourses in or anywhere near Orkney.' But I'm quite sure that few of these pub betters had ever visited a racecourse either, their little hobby, or iniquity (depending how you look at it) was exercised at a far remove from the scene of operations.

These reminiscences are prompted by Grand National day. Today, in every city of the south, the betting shops will be like beehives. But here in Orkney—apart from a few—nobody seems to care one way or the other; and betting on horses remains an activity almost as remote as opium eating.

'Pace' Eggs

18.4.1974

It's the day between Good Friday and Easter Sunday. On this day the town children, with baskets and tin cans, used to range about the countryside after 'pace eggs'. It was impossible to cover the whole parish of Stromness—Innertoon, Ootertoon, Quholm, Cairston, Kirbister, the Loons. You had to keep to one district; and then only visit farms where there were kindly women and tame dogs. You might come home with anything from six to a dozen eggs in your can, and all unbroken, if there was no fighting or bullying or horseplay on the road.

In some houses the eggs were boiled, and coloured in various hues; and on the Saturday or the Sunday there was a feast of 'pace eggs' and spicy hot cross buns. (There were probably chocolate eggs too, forty years ago, but they were not the large, glittering, opulent globes of the seventies.)

A lady anthropologist on the radio this morning was speaking about the tie-up between Easter and eggs. It is a very ancient ceremony of gifts, with traditions going back further than Christianity, and seemingly universal in the ancient world. The egg is never so plentiful as at this time of year; and to the first tribes of the world it symbolised the life of springtime when the apparently inert egg broke open to reveal a new bird. Christianity was always wise enough not to try to stamp out those beautiful ceremonies and beliefs. They identified the symbolism of the broken egg with the Resurrection. The tomb was breached and death was conquered.

So, when the peedie boys and lasses of Stromness ranged through the parish for 'pace eggs', what the kindly farm wives gave them was an Easter gift; a pledge that winter was at last over, and that soon the earth would be full of the plenitude of summer—young beasts, and birds, and growing oats—and the tide of ripeness would not stop till harvest. And after that there would be enough food in barn and cupboard to last through the darkness of another winter. Life was an endless celebration of death-and-renewal, darkness-and-light, barrenness-and-fruition...

How could we seven-year-olds coming home from the farms have known there was such meaning in a little hen's egg?

A Surplus of Books

25.4.1974

What can be done when the bookshelves begin to overflow with the mass of books I have accumulated over the past thirty years? One answer is to get a new bookcase, but there is hardly enough wall space for any more of them. Soon I will have to harden my heart and jettison a hundred or so. When I mention that it might come to that, some of my friends throw up horrified hands: oh, they could never bear to throw out books! But I have no particular attachment to books as such. To only about a hundred books am I thirled with any passion—I could go on reading them, quite happily, over and over again, for the rest of my days.

One of the authors I delight in is an old blind Argentinian called Jorge Luis Borges. He hasn't written much—only a handful of stories (some of them very short indeed) and a few poems. But they are so perfectly imagined and wrought that they are models of their kind. I was extremely pleased the other day, therefore, to get from Borges' translator, as a gift, two new books by the master—a new group of stories called *Doctor Brodie's Report* and *Borges on Writing*.

By an extraordinary coincidence the composer Peter Maxwell Davies, who is coming to settle in Rackwick soon, was in Buenos Aires. conducting and lecturing; and he met J. L. Borges by accident. Later they had a meal together and a long conversation. It turned out that the Norse Sagas are among Borges' favourite reading.

That is not to be wondered at—Borges is bound to admire the sheer narrative skill of the old Icelandic story tellers, who never wasted a word, who pared down their stories to the last syllable and the last letter.

So when Peter Maxwell Davies next came to Orkney, one of the first things he did was to get Charles Senior to despatch the Anderson

Orkneyinga Saga to Borges in the Argentine. How intriguing, to think of that great old man sitting back in his chair while somebody reads to him the story of the first Earl Rognvald and his dog in the seaweed at Papa Stronsay that terrible Yule; and of Sweyn Asleifson in a Dublin street with the sword-flashes all about him...

Film Fans

16.5.1974

How very sad, to read in last week's *Orcadian* about the Phoenix Cinema. I suppose I could count on my fingers the number of times I was there, not being a film fan. But the idea that a community like Orkney might soon be without a cinema is somehow dismaying. How much more so must it be to the real, devoted, dedicated film fans!

Forty years ago, in Stromness, we were all film fans. The cinema was the Town Hall. Price of admittance (for young folk) fourpence. Times of screening—Thursday and Saturday evenings.

Having accumulated, by whatever open or devious means, four pennies (and that was no easy matter in the lean thirties) you sat with other boys in the front two rows of that ugly building, chattering and sometimes fighting (but all such little forest fires were quickly douched by the attendant on duty). The seats behind slowly filled up with adults, admittance ninepence and one-and-three. It was a real social occasion. When a particularly popular citizen entered and took his seat, there was cheering and stamping of the feet.

Then—O marvellous moment!—the lights dimmed, and the ugly Town Hall became a cave of enchantment. Beams of shifting light from the hidden projector struck the screen, a cock gave a rousing salute, and the evening's entertainment began with Pathe Gazette— Herr Hitler's visit to Signor Mussolini, the fall of yet another French government, Mr Ramsay MacDonald driving from the first tee at Lossiemouth; and rather boring stuff like that. All the same, it was an appetiser for the delights to come.

Impossible, in such short space, to list all those delights—cowboys, molls, gangsters, boxers, sailors. A few films made such an impact that, forty years on, I can remember scenes from them vividly, and recapture some of the emotion I felt. There was that film about the Battle of Jutland, for example—the Town Hall was crowded that night! Most clearly and excitingly of all I recall a film about eighteenth-century highwaymen, in which the hero was an actor called Matheson Lang. In the end he was captured, tried, and sentenced. What superb tragedy as, in the open cart, that brave one whom the fates had treated scurvily went on to Tyburn! I have never felt such pathos since...

It often happened, of course, that the film broke down more than once in an evening, and then the cave of dark enchantment turned once more into the dingy lit-up Town Hall. How we roared with rage and bafflement then! But presently, with a whirr and a dimming of lights, the magic returned.

A Book on Golf

23.5.1974

How pleasant to have yet another small book about Stromness, and from the pen of ex-Provost George S. Robertson who last year gave us his *History of Stromness*—a nostalgic and well-documented account of all the trades, businesses, professions along the street within living memory.

Mr Robertson's new book is more specialised—it concentrates on that pastime that has been a devouring interest in his life: Golf.

Where the rabbits have burrowed since the start of time; where the peaceful dead of Stromness sleep in their countless thousands; where once lead was mined and more recently uranium has been located— there, at Warbeth, was the first Stromness Golf Course of nine sporting holes. There on a summer evening the golfers of the town (mostly then professional people) and their long-skirted ladies smote the gutta-percha with their baffies, and the still air resounded with loud irregular 'clacks'.

Warbeth must have been a delightful little course. But it lay miles from the town. In 1924 the Golf Club moved to its new 18-hole course at Ness. How the change came about is wonderingly and amusingly told by Mr Robertson: for the purchase of Ness Farm was triggered off by the sheerest accident, a chance meeting on the street between himself and Bailie T. R. Mowat, and the exchange of a few fruitful words.

After the Golf Club acquired the farm, hard and heroic labour was called for to convert what had for centuries been tilth-and-pasture into a golf course. Mr Robertson himself—though he never says so—was one of those who applied unstinted labour and ingenuity to the transformation. In 1924 it was a bold, risky venture. But fortune smiled; and today half a century later Stromness is fortunate indeed to possess one of the best little courses in the land; from the scenic aspect (Mr Robertson argues) the finest of all.

It was a story well worth telling. Mr Robertson's enthusiasm for golf spills over into his account: the unique story is told with verve and humour and deep affection.

This book[1] is a 'must' for the growing band of 'Orkney Book' collectors. It has a lively preface by Archie Bevan; a dozen unique and historic photographs; and notes on the other Orkney golf courses.

Forty Alehouses

30.5.1974

Somebody said, wonderingly, at the Pier Head one sunny afternoon this week, 'They tell me there were once forty pubs in Stromness!' And somebody else remarked, 'Every second door must have been a pub'...

It's quite true that when Rev Peter Learmonth wrote his *Statistical Account* in 1842, there were over forty places in Stromness where

---

1 *A History of the Stromness Golf Courses* by G. S. Robertson, JP, Provost of Stromness 1946-53. Printed by W. R. Rendall, Stromness, and published by the author.

drink could be bought. But most of these premises would not have been 'pubs' as we understand them. They would have been 'ale houses', where you drank the ale that was brewed on the premises. You would come in and sit in a decent parlour, and the good wife would bring you a pewter mug with a blown cap of foam atop, for which you would pay maybe a penny.

There would have been forty different varieties of ale to choose from along the street, a lovely thought in these latter days when all kinds of beer seem to taste, increasingly, the same. Also there would have been a complete scale of quality of house from Login's Inn at the top to some unspeakable grog-shop up some filthy close.

In Login's Inn at the South End, I imagine, the really important folk foregathered—the bailies, the merchants, the skippers. They would spill snuff out of enamelled boxes on to the back of their hands, and call for 'the waters' (by which they might mean brandy, rum, gin, or malt whisky). They would discuss grave matters of the day—such as, whether the proposed railroad between Stromness and Kirkwall was feasible; or, would the quarrying of granite at Brinkie's Brae be a profitable concern?... Occasionally a sovereign would glitter and birl in the till.

At the other extreme, in the nameless house up the filthy close, you would have to grope your way to a seat beside a barrel. And some old hag would whisper evilly into your ear, asking 'What's your pleasure?' And then, having got your ha'penny, she would tap the barrel. Shadows came and went across the webbed window. Everywhere were the stink and the feel of decay, and the ale was foul.

But mostly, I imagine, the average ale house of Stromness a hundred years ago was the decent parlour kept by a cleanly hard-working body, who took a pride in her ale. There might have been a framed text, or a sampler, on the wall...

'My goodness,' said a third speaker at the Pier Head, 'what a grand Saturday night you could have had in Stromness in them days!'

James MacTaggart, TV Drama Director

6.6.1974

It was sad to hear, on television news a few days ago, that James MacTaggart had died. He was only 45. Stromness folk will remember, two autumns ago, the hordes of actors and the television team that invaded the town, pleasantly. They are bound to remember James MacTaggart the director, a rather short thick-set man who was the most dominant character of them all. He had to be, for it was he who ruled their smallest gesture and word, when they were on the set; and arranged, with infinite patience, cameras and microphones.

To be a television drama director, especially on location in a place like Orkney notorious for its vagaries of weather, calls for courage, patience, and a high degree of organisational skill.

James MacTaggart and his actors and technicians arrived in September to make their three films[1]. September—as Orcadians know—is one of the ficklest months, liable to gales and lashings of rain. James MacTaggart decided, typically, to tackle the most difficult film first, the one set in Rackwick. The first two days were a continuous deluge of rain. I thought even he would have to beat a retreat. Not so—the filming went on—and all concerned arrived back in Stromness soaked in rain and spray, but all exhilarated and somehow enchanted. A few of them, including the director, got bad colds out of the experience; but Stromness is a good medical centre, and none of them was the worse. Fortunately, they had some good weather before the Rackwick film was completed.

I admired James MacTaggart's complete dedication. In the evening the actors could relax with books and talk and drink. Not this director; after dinner he retired to his room to plot, meticulously, the next day's filming. If he got five minutes' satisfactory filming out of a long day's shooting—and the same small scene might have to be done over and over again—he expressed himself satisfied. It must have been frustrating for all concerned when a whole day's filming at 'The White Horse' (Alfred Street) was in the end deleted. Another whole day was spent in 'The Arctic Whaler'—at Dr Mary Peace's in

1 *A Time to Keep—Celia—The Whaler's Return* (from three short stories out of my book *A Time to Keep* (Hogarth Press—1969)).

Dundas Street—only a few beautiful fragments were left—much that was worthwhile had to be sacrificed to the exigencies of time and form.

When he did relax, James MacTaggart was the greatest fun. His singing of 'Sing me a Hebridean Song, Daddy' was unforgettably droll and comic. And he enjoyed Orkney and its people and way of life.

There was a bit of filming that went on all night, and involved Fulton Mackay, Hannah Gordon, and Roddy MacMillan. That was at Flaws's Pier at the South End. There was an eerie beauty in the scene, as the same piece of enraged dialogue was repeated over and over, with Brian Tufano perilously poised with his camera above the shifting sea. They had to wait for the last scene till the dawn came up over Orphir. Alas, it was a grey, unspectacular sunrise; but James MacTaggart and his men were so good that even that (so I'm told by folk in the south who saw it on colour TV) was beautiful...

Temples of Science

13.6.1974

I read in yesterday's *Orcadian* Mrs Susan Flint's horrifying account of what might happen if something went wrong in Flotta—'instant roast beef' on our charred hillsides instead of the beautiful wandering cows 'like queens with their coats of silk'...

I suppose it does us all good, from time to time, to be shaken out of our complacency. We tend to accept too easily the marvels of science and technology—we accept them with complacency—it wouldn't be too much to say that we bestow on them the awe and reverence that wiser generations reserved for their divinities. Nobody can say yet just how dearly we shall have to pay, in terms of pollution and (what might be worse) a kind of withering of the human spirit, for all the affluence and ease we are splurging in now.

When first the silver sphere of Dounreay began to glint in the sun from the other side of the Pentland Firth, half a generation ago, I was sitting at the Pier Head with an old fisherman; now, alas, dead—he was one of the best storytellers I have known, and when he was laid in the kirkyard at last a great treasury of local lore was buried with him. His name was John Folster.

We might have been waiting at the Pier Head for the bar to open, so that we could have our morning beer, or maybe we were just enjoying the sunshine. Somehow, the name Dounreay was mentioned. John Folster shook his head solemnly. He could see that Temple of Science every day, fishing for haddocks round the Kame of Hoy. 'If that goes up,' he said, 'there'll be no Orkney left—nothing but cinders in the sea!' ... I remember having a secret smile to myself, thinking it was the groundless fears of an old traditional fisherman who trusted nothing but the tides, the drift of fish, and his own sea-skills.

But when one reads of the frightful danger that resides even in the waste material of such places, and how it might have to he buried for a millennium before it can be pronounced safe—I wonder now if John Folster's fears might have come out of some deep ancestral wisdom.

Of course Dounreay will never 'go up', in John Folster's sense. The real danger is that the human mind has somehow been wrenched out of its frame by a sovereignty that may be only partly well-disposed to us; and, for all we know, may yet show itself positively hostile.

A Lost Letter

27.6.1974

'For a week and more before the big night,' some Innertown crofter might have written 150 years ago (only it is unlikely he had ever attended one of the score of schools in Stromness) 'we had gathered anything and everything that would burn and we had made a big pile of driftwood and heather on Farafield Hill. It was an anxious night or two, for there were heavy clouds in the west, and we didn't want the pile to get wet.

'The women weren't idle, I assure you. They had been brewing for weeks. Now they were making oatcakes and bannocks and cheese ready.

'Young and old were eagerly looking forward to Johnsmas eve. I'm thankful to say it was a fine day on the 23rd. After sunset, late in the evening, everybody in the district who could manage went to the fire. It was set alight by the oldest man there. Just after the first flames he did a thing that made us all laugh and hold our breath at the same time. In a very secret manner he took an animal bone out of his coat pocket and dropped it into the heart of the fire. Then he had to step back quickly or he would have been choked with the gathering reek.

'Then it was the turn of the young men. Some of them were showing off in front of the girls, to demonstrate what fine brave fellows they were. One after the other they leapt through the fire. It was very important, even the "show-offs" knew that this fire-jump should be done by as many as possible. Of course after a time the smoke and heat were too great. Then the young men and women had to content themselves with dancing round the fire. I suppose most of them found that even more enjoyable than the jumping.

'It was a very fine sight, about midnight, to see a dozen other fires burning on hilltops far and near. All the countryfolk of Orkney were rejoicing in the same way as we were.

'I was keeping my eye on my father. Soon after midnight he went up to the fire and from it he lit a torch he had carefully prepared. He went home quickly then along the road. There were flickers here and there throughout the district. The other crofters were doing the same. Once they got home, each man would carry the lighted torch through his field, and into barn, stable, byre, house. They seemed to think the torches would cleanse and enrich and protect their crofts.

'If you ask me why all these fires were lit on midsummer's eve, I cannot tell you. All I know is, it's a very old custom. The minister and some of the merchants and townsfolk are in favour of doing away with it, but we countryfolk wouldn't be without our Johnsmas fires. We believe—at least the old ones still do, I have doubts about it myself—that if the fires weren't lit the crops would fail and the animals would perish, and there would be famine. I remember a very old farmer saying when I was a boy that we had to thank the kindly sun for ripening our crops and we had to do it with our smaller fires and with our sunward dancings. There was also, he said, a hidden fire at the centre of the earth that warmed the roots of oat and bere, and it too was honoured by our fire ceremony.

'But that was just an old superstitious man speaking. It's possible, indeed likely, that in years to come folk will take a more sober, commonsensical view of agriculture as knowledge and education grow...'

John Firth Countryside

11.7.1974

Still more Orkney books. Recently there has been Edwin Muir's *Selected Letters*—I suppose one can call it an Orkney book, though there are only random references to Orkney. But the remarks he lets drop about his childhood in Orkney are profound and beautiful: they are the seeds of his *The Story and the Fable* (later retitled *An Autobiography*) and his poems. I hope somebody like E.W.M[1] will give this important book the treatment it deserves in some future issue of this paper.

For those who have only heard about the classic *Reminiscences of An Orkney Parish* by John Firth, or who have only handled it with reverence in the library, it must surely be good news that it has been reissued, in photostat form, by the Stromness Museum, with additional notes and photographs; and in two formats, hardback and paperback... By chance, going to visit friends[2] who have rented a cottage at the side of the beautiful Lyde Road the other day, the car I was in passed right through the very district of Redland that John Firth wrote about with such care and devotion. It was one of those marvellous summer afternoons that have been gifted to us so lavishly in 1974, with great white clouds and rich light over everything. The owner of the car was an Edinburgh publisher, who is also a fine photographer. He couldn't waste an afternoon like that. We put in at a layby and he angled his camera here and there. Obligingly a pony

1 Ernest W. Marwick, Orkney historian and scholar.
2 Brian and Eliza Murray, Ayr.

strolled up the steep field and put her head over the gate to greet us; so she became part of some photographs, and she seemed to think it adequate reward to get in return fistfuls of juicy clover-fragrant grass from the ditch (we carried no sugar or sweeties). Then the little dark foal missed its mother—it came stumbling up the field, shy and uncertain; and its advent made even more interesting compositions...

How fortunate, I thought, John Firth's crofters of a hundred years ago were to be living in such a beautiful place. But the sombre thought always follows that beauty (at least self-conscious admiration of sea and earth and sky) did not enter into their scheme of things. It was in a far more rooted and potent sense that these generations of Orkney peasants were a part of the landscape they lived in.

The True Story of Phin the Soldier

18.7.1974

Mr R. P. Fereday's essay on Phin the Irish drummer is splendid. About this time last year, prompted by tourists I was going round the parishes in a car with, I indulged my imagination on the subject of Phin; and next week reproduced the fantasy in this column. Now I am more than glad to have the sober facts.

What can one say about Phin after reading Mr Fereday's account? He must have been tough. Only a robust man could have come through all those years of active service in the Napoleonic Wars; if you escaped the sabres and the balls, all kinds of diseases were lying in wait for you. Phin's sole incapacity was a hernia.

Phin was an intelligent man. He knew how to write a letter, with an authentic seasoning of Irish magniloquence in it. Only once does he fall into incoherence, and that is when he is upbraiding John Miller of the Mill for his injustice and uncharity.

He was an unfortunate man, alas. After all those many adventures, he might have hoped, like Ulysses, to settle in peace for the rest of his life above the Oyce of Firth, landlord of the ale house there—on good terms with everyone, and with a free and fair understanding between

163

himself and John Miller, the great man of the district. Mr Fereday speculates, and rightly I'm sure, that the farmers and crofters of Firth who dropped in to the ale house to quench their thirsts, must have been enchanted with Phin. An Irish storyteller ranks high in the scale of this world's entertainers. Phin had a wealth of adventure to pour out to his customers; and what if occasionally he mingled some fantasy and whimsy with authentic accounts of battle and siege and forced march? It was more than an ale house too—you could have bought, secretly, a dram in a dark corner. That is why, surely, the establishment got its name, The Toddy Hole.

John Miller put an end to the idyll very soon.

John Miller was one of those powerful characters, mentally and physically, that get thrown up from time to time to trouble an easy-going community. (He reminds me of Gourlay in *The House with the Green Shutters*.) His bitter feud with Phin, after the affable beginning, makes painful reading. It all began because a boy—Phin's son—made a bit of a noise one day around the Mill of Firth.

The real founder of the village in Firth parish is rightly John Miller, Mr Fereday says. The place should be Millertoon. Time brings in his subtle revenges. Poor Phin, handled more roughly by Miller than ever he had been in his long years of campaigning, disappeared into the shadows. But it continued to be 'Phin's' that the Firth folk and travellers dropped into to wet their throats. When the village was big enough for a name they called it Finstown. Thus it was the Irish soldier, and not 'the little tyrant of the fields', who got the immortality.

Cocktails Afloat

1.8.1974

It had been cold for July all day, and for days past (not like the generous early summer at all). There was a fitful gleam of cold sunlight as we climbed aboard the *Hamnavoe*. As the *Hamnavoe* made for the mouth of the harbour an immense blue-black cloud launched itself from the northwest, and we crossed Hoy Sound blind with rain.

But by the time we reached RFA *Stromness*, lying in the Bring Deeps between Graemsay and Hoy, there were splashes of wan sunlight again.

But oh, that ship's ladder we had to climb! It was steep and it seemed to soar into the clouds. Through every open rung, as up I went, I could glimpse snarling, ugly sea far below. To one who is troubled with agoraphobia on a firm street on a fine day, it was a nightmare ascent.

But at last it was over—we were all gathered on the deck, and were kindly welcomed by the officers of the ship. And all at once, it seemed, we were surrounded by a swarm of small Chinese waiters, efficient and unobtrusive, asking mutely what our pleasure was. I thought I would try some gin for a change, with a sliver of lemon in it. All around generous liquid welcome was being decanted.

All the officers; from the captain down, were pleasant and friendly, and seemed, without willing it, to keep the little groups swirling everywhere, so that there was no time to get tired of anyone's company, and everyone must have spoken to everyone else before the evening was over... And always, at your elbow when your glass showed signs of being empty, stood a little oriental, smiling, deferential, eager to please.

To tell the truth I was still shaken by that airy fearful diagonal climb up the ship's side. I thought that going down would be an even more frightful experience. It put a cloud over the whole evening. It became a question then of drinking sufficient gin-and-lemon to give me courage; but not a surfeit that might plunge me head first to a watery grave in Burra Sound. Again, after half an hour, the inscrutable smile beside me, and the golden hand held out for my empty glass.

At one side, on an immense table, stretched a delectable buffet; sandwiches of all kinds, curry pies, chicken pies, endless cheeses, biscuits, cakes. We ate discreetly and well—I washed mine down with the clean taste of gin.

It was time to go. As it happened, I descended the steps on a cloud of euphoria, and wished it had been far, far longer. When all were on board, the launch eased itself into the bitterness of Burra Sound and headed for Stromness.

The Show Season

8.8.1974

The 'Show Season' is on us once more. How quickly the cycle of the year turns! Tomorrow, with any luck, I'll be setting out with thousands of others for that famous show at Dounby, in the very centre of the West Mainland.

There are so many happy memories of Dounby Shows over the years, that not even the deluges that all but washed out the past two shows can soil them.

I know that it is meant to be a showpiece for the animals of seven parishes—and superb beasts they are, sleek and woolly and powerful, and marvellously groomed. But for a townee like me the people are even more entrancing.

Eric Linklater had a splendid description, in *Whitemaa's Saga*, of the folk crowding into either a Lammas Market or the County Show in Kirkwall almost half a century ago. The same folk, in all their variety, will be at Dounby tomorrow; only they will be a bit more prosperous, and the young folk will be a bit taller and more stylishly dressed, and the animals will be even more magnificent. (Such is the paradox of our times, that when everybody is complaining about depression, inflation, stagnation, all the outward signs point to affluence as never before. Any eye that can span forty years, coldly, will tell you the same.)

Well, then, may the Dounby Show be blessed this year with sunshine and tumultuous crowds. Here, if anywhere, it is possible to see, gathered into one small field, a swatch of the typical Orkney—laird, merchant, farmer, seaman, countrywoman, student, bairn...

If I try to think of any one happy Dounby Show out of the past, it is almost impossible, for all those August days unfold like a single fan covered with gay patterns. Even when the gate is finally closed in the show park, and the patient beasts are loaded for home, the day keeps an afterglow. I remember sitting at the end of a cottage in the evening sun, beside the Loch of Harray, drinking delicious home brew—then being driven back to Stromness while the stoical stanzas of Housman and Hardy were quoted across the car. And I got a bag full of new potatoes, fat juicy mushrooms, a dew-filled lettuce, to keep me going in the following days.

And there was the evening with Roger, Debby and a German student when we played records of Beethoven and Dylan Thomas, and recited passages out of books, till two or three in the morning. But that must have been another Dounby Show...

The Summer School of Music

22.8.1974

One of the most astonishing things about the Stromness calendar is the concert given each August at the end of the week-long Orkney Orchestral Summer School. It is something of a miracle that children are willing to forego the outdoor joys of summer—the beaches and piers and boats—to devote themselves to an intensive course of musical study, practice and performance. And most days last week, when the summer school was in session, were bright and warm. Yet there they were, with their violins and clarinets and trumpets, going to their practice, making themselves ready for the final flowering—the concert on the last night.

To us of another generation, it showed vividly the progress that school music has made of recent years. We remember, with a shudder, that bleak hour once a week, with the endless ear-tests and the incomprehensible staff notations scrawled across the blackboard. By way of relief, we were launched occasionally into a chorus or two—'Sir Eglamore, that worthy Knight' or 'See afar yon hill Ardmore'...

In the meantime, thank goodness, there has been a drastic revolution. In no small measure the change has come about because of the talent and drive and enthusiasm of Mrs Jean Leonard and her assistants. For six years past, too, a team of able musicians and music teachers from the south, under Mr Roy Lennox, have come to Orkney to put a final polish on the skills of those young performers.

I happened to walk into the Community Centre one morning when a practice was taking place. Apart from the obvious joy of the children in the music they were giving out, I couldn't help wondering at the organisation that went into everything. (But joy in a task imposes its own willing discipline.) And then it was no elementary pieces that they were tackling. There were two movements of a Beethoven symphony, for example; there was a specially composed 'Peedie Suite for Brass', by one of the brass tutors, Robert Stein. The young musicians had seen all the scores, for the first time, only a few days before.

The single performance on Thursday evening was highly successful. The Community Centre was packed to the doors—with parents, tourists and folk who just liked music.

Amid much that is depressing in society these days, the opening of the 'magic casements' of music to young hands and imaginations is a very wonderful thing.

Old Maps

5.9.1974

There's this delight in poring over old maps, with all their crudities, inaccuracies, naiveties. Modern maps don't give anything like the same pleasure—they are too coldly correct and infallible.

In Charles Senior's shop the other day—that treasure trove—I bought for 25p 'A Map of Orkney Shire, drawn from the best Authorities by T. Kitchin'. There's no date, but it seems to come from well back in the eighteenth century. It seems possible also from the inscription that the cartographer was never in Orkney at all, but did his best by consulting older maps. Maybe an old seaman or two in Leith told him some things. (It was printed in Edinburgh.)

T. Kitchin depicts hills on his map by means of stylised little humps, all of the same size exactly. The hills of Hoy are no bigger or smaller than the hills of Holm. But there is an attempt at some kind of accuracy—the flat islands, Sanday, North Ronaldsay, Flotta, have no 'humps'.

The shapes of the islands approximate to what we know them to be. T. Kitchin was far more accurate than Johan Blaeu whose map of the year 1654 has many ludicrous things in it. Slowly science is taking over from guesswork and legend. But even so, Hoy (for example) is far too long and narrow. And there are only two lochs, 'Stenes Loughs'. And 'Graham Hall' (presumably Graemeshall) is set firmly on Scapa beach.

The place names are most fascinating of all: 'Sanda', 'Birsa', 'Westra', 'Burra'. It seems more than likely that our forefathers did indeed pronounce them in that way. We moderns have inherited a corruption from later map-makers; which is why we say and write 'Kirkwall' instead of 'Kirkvoe'. I'm glad to see that T. Kitchin eschewed 'Pomona', the most lamentable error of all.

This brings us to Stromness. The growing village is marked 'Cairston' on this map. There is 'Strom Ness', too, in the vicinity, but it is a headland somewhere in the vicinity of Breckness or the Black Craig... The early Stromnessians were clearly undecided what to call their home town—Cairston, Hamnavoe, Stromness. In the end they decided—perhaps, again, with the help of cartographers—on the least interesting alternative.

This map of T. Kitchin is a thing of delight. What a work of art it is, too, with its elegant tints and embellishments.

Our Happiest Days

19.9.1974

I am trying to envisage a school on the Garson shore.

Forty years ago, the time to get up for a schoolboy was roughly 8.30am. There was no bedroom clock—you were shouted on from downstairs. You stretched it out for five more drowsy, delicious minutes. Meantime the shouts from the foot of the stairs became ever more dire and hectoring.

Well, there were no ablutions. Face-washing had been done the night before. (I have heard of young ones who even took their cornflakes before retiring, to be ready for that hectic morning dash to school...)

Where have they vanished to, those delicious rolls that the cookie-boy used to leave on the front doorstep every morning? They're not making them like that any more. They were long, and they had a kind of depression in the floury centre of them. Spread thick with butter from the farm of Citadel—and devoured between table and door—you were ready to face another day. (And where in this drab world of the seventies is there such creaminess and mellowness to be found as in that butter from the farm at the back of the town?)

Ready to face another day? That's a piece of false hindsight, if you like. With your tattered schoolbag under your arm—and books and jotters threatening every minute to spill out—you set out. And as you hurried along, you meditated miserably on the homework not done, or done in such a slapdash fashion that there was bound to be trouble. Also on the timetable ahead, a dreary patchwork of maths and Latin and geography.

But you were not alone, that was one consolation. As you hurried along Ness Road and through the South End and along the twistings of Alfred Street and Dundas Street, you were joined by 'other souls in pain', sleep in their eyes and mouths smeared with syrup-and-crumbs. It was a troop of Dantean figures that turned up Khyber Pass for the final climb to the Academy.

Quite often some sadistic adult in a doorway would shout at us, 'You'd better hurry up!' (As if we didn't know.) Would we, by some miracle, arrive in time? It had, on a rare occasion, been known to happen. But there, somewhere between the hearse shed and the top of Kirk Road, the bell began. Of all the dolorous noises I have heard on this earth, that bell of Stromness Academy takes some beating...

Another day had got off to a bad start. Dire predictions were made, by those in authority, as to our future careers, and the downward graphs thereof. Then the tawse was brought out.

How will it he, for a south-ender, in 1984, when his 'alma mater' is on the other side of the bay?

The Autumn Equinox

26.9.1974

The autumn equinox is almost here—I'm writing this on September 20. There's a solemnity still in those turning points of the year, solstices and equinoxes; for of course we no longer accord them the veneration that earlier Orcadians thought fitting at such cardinal dates of the calendar.

If only we could read the great stone book of Brodgar! It was undoubtedly erected with some reference to, and reverence for, the waxing and waning of the fruitful year. We do know that the setting sun on the winter solstice sends a fleeting gleam through the long passageway of Maeshowe, and touches (for the only time in the bright year) the wall of entombment. It is like a golden seed sown in the heart of darkness. There is some notion here of resurrection, we may be sure. Here is a mystery that catches the breath. We have at least to revise our opinion of those 'ignorant savage' ancestors of ours. They were men of great skill and sensitivity—that much is certain. They were poets in stone. Their bodies responded vividly to changes of light and darkness, in a way that those of television viewers don't. We have lost a great deal in the last two centuries—maybe too much— for a few tawdry benefits.

Midsummer in Orkney is still a wonderful time even though we light no more Johnsmas fires. And round about 21st March is a season of marvellous quickening: one can feel the great wave of light bursting over the islands.

Theoretically, the winter solstice ought to be a season of gloom and hopelessness. But here men have always placed their most joyous festivals—Yule, Saturnalia, Christmas. Undoubtedly the architect of genius who built Maeshowe, so that the last seed of the sun was safely hoarded in that chamber of death, was moved by the same spirit of relief and joy. The great darkness was not going to go on until the earth was nothing but a clot of blackness and ice. The chamber is womb-shaped, and with a reason; out of it would come next year's increase.

No, it is this autumn equinox that is the saddest time of the year. The summer is over—we are about to enter the long, cold, dark tunnel. Shadows cluster about the mind and the spirit. But even here men found reasons for rejoicing. The harvest was over; earth had yielded her fruits. In snug barns, all over Orkney for many centuries, fiddles were tuned and the ale went from mouth to happy mouth... I think sometimes it is because of these festivities that the human race has endured for so long.

A Good Teacher

24.10.1974

It was sad to hear of the death of Mr John Shearer. To most Orcadians he was the ex-Director of Education, but our generation in Stromness remember him as the science master at Stromness Academy in the thirties.

Many a classroom we entered in those days with trepidation, or mere boredom. But it was always a pleasure to know that there was a science period ahead. 'The Lab', looking east over the rooftops of Stromness and the Cairston Roads, was dominated by an amiable presence. There was something immensely attractive about John Shearer, for children; it was possibly his humour, his patience, his kindness, his interest in every individual pupil, no matter how dull or unattractive he or she might be. I think, in short, he was gifted with the kind of 'charity' mentioned in scripture.

It's a fact, I suppose—and very natural—that some teachers are interested only in the pupils who are good at their particular subject. Life is short, knowledge is precious—it is impossible for most teachers to cater for everybody... John Shearer wasn't that kind of teacher. I was very stupid when it came to physics and chemistry— every experiment in which I participated seemed to end in disaster. At length I was entrusted merely with the weighing of crucibles etc on those infinitely delicate scales when you had to pick up the fraction-of-a-milligram weights with tweezers, for finger-sweat might make a difference. (Any fool could do it.) I ought, therefore, to have been a 'second-class pupil', hardly worth bothering with. But John Shearer is the teacher I always recall with affection—he showed me endless patience and consideration and pleasantness. And he put the same kind glow on all his pupils, clever or dull, clean or ragged, rich or poor.

I think his sense of justice too appealed to us all. He never flew into rages; any alleged trespass he considered gravely, for a long time, stroking his chin between thumb and forefinger. And then when at last the verdict came, it was always accepted without question—even, on a very rare occasion, the tawse.

He had a fine sense of humour also—his teaching was interspersed with jokes (chiefly of the 'schoolboy howler' type) and with reminiscences of his youthful service in the First World War... It was always pleasant just to sit and let that amiable, gentle, mellow voice flow over us. He seems to me now, looking back, to have been the essence of all that was good in the Orkney way of life.

The Dweller in the Tall Red House

7.11.1974

There is a telephone box just below the window. It fits snugly into a corner of the Museum. All the people of the South End use it—there's no other public phone till you come to the Post Office; beyond that, there are a couple at the Pier Head.

It is, as I said, a much-used telephone. Often enough, when you want to phone, you see somebody else inside. I have seen, in evenings in summer, quite a crowd lingering around it. (Nobody in Orkney likes forming a queue.)

In former times you had to wait long enough while some loquacious body rattled on about Aunty Bella's rheumatics, how the rhubarb jam turned out this year, and peedie Tam was getting on fine with his arithmetic now, thank goodness... But the phone at the corner of the Museum has ceased to be indulgent with such gossips; it recently turned quite business-like. Three minutes' talking for two pence, that was all. I have been left gaping like a fish myself, after the three minutes, my single two pence swallowed up in the silence.

It is a very cheerful phone. Sometimes you hear it ringing away merrily, as if it was warbling to itself. One day last week it was chortling like that—I was on my way to the shops. I sidestepped into the kiosk, but just as I was reaching out to lift the receiver, it stopped. I'm sure it must have seen me coming.

Some awful things have been done to that happy phone over the past months. The worst thing of all was when it was ripped out by the roots. That happened—I think—at last winter's end. One feels a little chill of apprehension when such senseless violence is done. It is like a ripple from those mindless football mobs in Glasgow, Manchester, London.

A few weeks ago one of the thick glass panes was smashed. Now, until it's mended, you have to phone in a cold draught.

On Hallowe'en I ought, of course, to have known better. I was making two local telephone calls. I had to tell my friends to speak up, their voices were so thin and far off. It was only when I was putting down the receiver that I noticed the smear of treacle on my hand. The whorls of my ear felt sticky too. Some Hallowe'en revellers had douched the earpiece of the phone with that dark, plebeian honey...

I suppose it is mild enough fun, compared with some Hallowe'en capers. But I can't help thinking it might have been some old or infirm body wanting something urgently—medical aid, say... Not to speak of the indignity done to that cheerful and popular presence, the dweller in the tall red house.

In the Kitchen

14.11.1974

There must be at least ten thousand recipes in the western world, judging by the proliferation of cookery books and articles on the subject in magazines. Some houses you visit are stacked with gastronomic literature. How on earth, you think, is any housewife, however adventurous in the kitchen, going to provide her man and her children with any but the smallest fraction of those recipes?

For bachelors who have to look after themselves the problem is simpler. For some of them it is solved by buying tins of this and that, and packets of this and that, from the grocer's. Even mashed tatties come in powdered form now. A firm tried tinned porridge, but that did not work. There might be problems with tinned ham-and-eggs, too.

But eating out of tins is no fun at all. It is cheating in a way. There is a great satisfaction in really cooking a good meal in your own kitchen for yourself. It's much simpler than I thought, too. A few years ago I could maybe brew a pot of tea and boil an egg and fry a kipper. But that was all. I have learned over the years to make the most delicious broth, and stews that melt in the mouth. I'm still not happy with roasts or casseroles; and when I try to fry fish half the skin and the ruskoline remain in the pan. These are mysteries I must solve some time.

Soup, mince, eggs, stew, kippers—it is not a large repertoire. A sophisticated palate would quickly grow tired of the monotony. Still, it's wonderful how you can manage, week by week, on such basic menus (especially when kind friends invite you to their houses at weekends to share in delicious roasts, curries, kedgerees).

When I got up the other morning it was very wintry. There was a virgin packet of porridge oats somewhere in the cupboard. The first attempt was a failure—thick lumpy stodge. Next morning it was as thin as the milk I poured over it. But now my porridge, well salted, is as good as anything you would get in the Ritz.

I had a visit from a delightful American girl in the autumn who taught me how to make omelettes, either with cheese, bacon, tomatoes, mushrooms. Now I have omelette for dinner at least once a week, with bread and butter. I still bless the day when Gail took the whisk to the broken eggs in the bowl one Monday evening in my kitchen, and shredded the cheese and sliced the tomatoes, and heated the pan till it sizzled... I have, I admit, some difficulty in folding the flaps of the omelette over its savoury centre. Some day soon, by dint of trying, I may be able to fasten the fragrant envelope satisfactorily.

A New Ferry Boat

21.11.1974

I must be the last Stromnessian to board the new *St Ola*. To make my meaning clear. I haven't boarded her yet. Yesterday (Thursday) was the day for the general public; but yesterday I was housebound with a cold and, seeing that it was a nasty kind of day, I thought I'd better not risk turning that cold into pleurisy or pneumonia. I sat in the rocking-chair beside the fire and had a couple of toddies.

This morning I saw as I went shopping—and still sniffling and wheezing (but the cupboard must be replenished)—swarms of schoolchildren climbing the gangway. Perhaps I could lose myself in one of these groups? Greyness and wrinkles assort ill with the apple-cheeks and fresh laughter of young folk...

I'll have a look through her some day soon, for sure.

It's difficult to convey the pride that Stromnessians have in their *Ola*. For them it is as much a part of the town as Brinkie's Brae or Victoria Street. The *Ola* going out in the morning and returning in the afternoon is the proper heartbeat of the town. One gets the feeling that if Stromness were ever to be deprived of that ship, it would wither and die.

So, no wonder they have been smiling and nodding approval at the Pier Head ever since last Wednesday. The new *Ola* is here. It is an earnest that the life of the town will go on for another quarter of a century...

I am trying to remember what happened when the present ship—whose days are numbered—arrived in 1950... There was, for one thing, the spectacle of both *Ola*s, the mid-twentieth-century one and the Victorian one, entering the harbour together. That was a sight that took a lump to the throat of many a Stromnessian who had never shown emotion since he was a child!... And then there was a brief cruise through Scapa Flow—I remember that—I was there... And in the months following there were special Sunday trips—I remember a marvellous one that made a complete circle round Hoy. Many of us wouldn't mind doing that again.

Twenty years is not a long time in the history of a town. I may be wrong, but I have the feeling that the second *St Ola* never sank such deep roots into the heart of the community as her predecessor. What batterings she took in the Pentland Firth for sixty years! And yet, smooth passage or rough, there she entered the harbour every afternoon like a serene black swan. She would give her double salute to the town. And the town, hearing that heartbeat, would know that all was well.

The Hill behind Hamnavoe

28.11.1974

How one wastes time in vain speculation! A week or two back I fell to wondering idly about the name Brinkie's Brae, and what the origin of it was. I suppose many another Stromnessian must have been equally curious.

To while away a forenoon, I wrote an article for *The Scotsman*, full of whimsical guesses and suggestions. Brinkie, I assumed, must have been a man who lived a couple of centuries ago maybe. But why is the name all that is left of him? Why is he not framed in any legend? A name divorced from a story is highly unusual in a place like Orkney...

I went on to imagine a huge Irishman, called Byrne or O'Brien—one of the soldiers (like Phin of Finstown) who were stationed in Orkney after the Peninsular War. The Stromness contingent is said to have built those granite walls across the side of the hill... Or Brinkie might have been a hard-luck man—one of those unfortunates who are always on the brink, the verge, of some great achievement, but who never quite make it. This one returned from the nor-west with tales of gold mines and the daughters of Indian chiefs that had just eluded him.

The other day I got a pleasant letter from an Edinburgh man who had read that article. He quoted a child's rhyming game, which involved touching somebody on various parts of the face, beginning with the chin, and chanting:

Chin, chin, cherry.
Mou', mou', merry,
Nose, nose, nappy,
E'e, e'e, winkie,
Broo, broo, brinkie...

'It may be pure coincidence,' says my correspondent, 'as in so many of these philological matters, but one does refer to the brow of a hill (or brae). Anyway, I've never heard of any other *brinkie*.'...

It was a fascinating speculation. But if it is correct, one would expect the word to be in *The Orkney Norn*. But it isn't; it is a Scottish word entirely. It was while I was looking for *brinkie* in *The Orkney Norn* that my eye fell on the word *brinno*: 'a heather fire, fire on hill, any bright blazing fire...'

The derivation is the old Norse *brenna*, a fire.

Is this the simple explanation? It seems highly probable. All the Orkney hills were fire hills at the time of Beltane and Johnsmas; like Stromness's more modest elevation, 'vartha fiold' which we call today Farafield, or the Look-Out.

It was an amazing piece of stupidity on my part not to have looked into *The Orkney Norn*, years ago, for this explanation is most probably true.

Josie and the Ice Age

5.12.1974

Josie got his *Radio Times* one week and saw on the cover a huge wall of ice covering most of the northern hemisphere. Fascinated, he read the article inside; it seemed to suggest that a new Ice Age was overdue. Signs of it were the climatic changes happening everywhere—the desert expanding in Africa, the worsening weather in England, etc.

Unfortunately, Josie doesn't get BBC2 on his TV and it was too far to tramp across the valley in the rain to Albert's farm where they can get BBC2 (except that Albert's teenagers will have nothing, nightlong, but Grampian).

So Josie sat in his armchair, while Maggie knitted placidly on the other side of the fire, and read *The Orkney Book*. He read how the last Ice Age had covered the entire North Sea, including Orkney. It had gouged out the Hills of Hoy and littered the islands with 'boulder clay'. What on earth, Josie wondered, would things have been like at that time? Certainly there would have been no living things. Or was it possible a polar bear might occasionally have ambled across the whiteness where his oatfield and planticru were now? Fascinated, Josie read pieces out of the essay aloud. 'Fancy that!' said Maggie, and went on with her knitting. Before she went to bed she said, 'What's to come must just be tholed!'

Josie was deeply concerned. He had two extra bottles of home-brew before he went to bed, and (he ought to have known) slept in... When at last he got up and looked through the bedroom window, bleary-eyed, he saw something that made his breath flutter with panic. The black earth of his planticru was salted with snow!

He blundered downstairs and shouted to Maggie, 'It's coman. The Ice Age is on the wey! Hurry up, lass; we're gettan oot o' here!'

Maggie told him 'no to be a fooly brute' and eat his porridge. 'And anywey,' said she, 'whar'll we go tae?'

That was certainly a problem, for the Ice Age was to cover all of Britain except a tip of Cornwall.

'I wonder,' he mumbled through his porridge, 'could I learn to build an igloo? If the Eskimos can survive, Maggie, what's to stop us pokan holes in the ice and catchan a fish? And they've hunted walrus for hunders o' years...'

With great patience, Maggie said that the English had gotten into a bit of a panic because of their recent weather—a bad summer and a wet cold autumn. So, as is the fashion nowadays, they had let their minds hurtle to the bottom of the black well of pessimism...

Josie, eating his egg and bere bannock, thought there might be something in that indeed. He remembered the lovely mild winter to autumn that 1974 had been in Orkney. By the time he had drunk the last of his tea, he was quite cheerful... And when he went and opened the door, the genial sun of early winter had melted the rime in his planticru; the first white deathly whisper of the Ice Age!

Vanished Folk

9.1.1975

I was reading somewhere the other day about the 'Johnny Onions' who in prewar days used to tramp all over Scotland, with poles over their shoulders festooned with onions, selling their wares at every door. These Bretons came to Orkney too—inoffensive men, with berets on their heads and broken English. But, as the article I was reading said, they have not been seen since the end of the war. I fell to thinking about others who have disappeared from our streets and roads. The tinkers for one—a familiar sight in the closes of Stromness not so long ago.

There was 'the blind fiddler' who came every summer with the fairground folk, and was part of the enchantment of Lammastide. The kind of music he made, I suppose, will never return to the Pier Head and the Market Green.

Whenever the local fishermen in their little motorboats had a fair catch they poured the haddocks into an open barrow and sold them about the streets at sixpence a pound. There the thick fine silver fish hung from a little brass hand-scale before they were emptied into the housewife's basin. Cats and gulls mewed at every slipway when the wives gutted their fish and swilled them in the sea.

Winter was enriched by the lamplighter who went from gas lamp to gas lamp along the street with two poles, one to reach up and turn the gas tap, the other with a bead of light at the top of it to illumine the mantle. It is easy to romanticise this nightly ritual; it must have been an awkward job on a stormy winter night. The lamplighter had to go his round twice—the second time, after midnight, to darken the street again... His only reprieve was the few nights round about the full moon when (for economic reasons) the lamps weren't lit.

Other flame-bearers were the postmen (my father among them). The main delivery then was at night after the *Ola* had berthed; for of course it was before the time of airmail. Many a 'coorse night' the postmen had too. They read the addresses by the light of a lantern pinned to their coat lapels. They always had a cheery word in every doorway, fair weather or foul.

On Saturday nights the Salvation Army stood in a circle here and there—at the Pier Head, at the foot of Church Road, for example, with their songs, tambourines and trumpets. My mother used to do her shopping on a Saturday evening when I was a small boy. I went with her. The shops were open until eight or nine at night. The songsters, the crowd, the lighted shops, the Saturday poke of sweeties—all made the weekend a time of pure delight.

A Bed for Snow

16.1.1975

I think folk, in the days before BBC weather forecasting, used to be far more sensitive to impending changes in the weather. Many of the old ones, of course, worked by the calendar; there were the superstitions attaching to Candlemas, Beltane, St Swithin's, which hardly ever 'came up' with the predicted weather, but were adhered to nevertheless, year after year, by those ultra-conservatives. I remember, as a boy, being impressed by the weather-lore of the fishermen. They had to have great cunning as to the airt of wind and the phase of the moon, and what weather might be expected from such and such a conjunction; their livelihoods, even their lives, depended on it. So, seated at the fishermen's wall at the end of a long, warm July day, when it seemed that there could be no end to summertime, a fisherman would take his pipe out of his mouth and announce that tomorrow would be a day of rain. How scornful we were! How on earth could he see rain in that serene roseate evening sky? We would drift away, maybe, to catch sillocks. We would waken next morning, sure enough, to the lash of rain on the window pane; and the end of another brief summer idyll.

Now, in the early days of January, we wait for the traditional January weather: snow.

It may never come. 1974 was a mild snowless January. But usually, when an Orkneyman thinks of January, he says 'snow', and shivers.

There have been Januaries that obliterated everything in a huge dazzling whiteness. Roads were blocked, crofts half-buried. Still the snow fell, billions and trillions of flakes, in a slow, hushed trance. The electricity failed one January; out came the old cobwebby paraffin lamps that were never meant to be lit again, but were kept 'just in case'.

We learned again, by candlelight, to listen to each other's voices. We experienced something of the old primitive dread of winter... But these tremendous snowfalls seem to be the exception nowadays.

Every day, as I go along the street, I am waiting to hear some old body say, 'It's a bed for snow'... What constitutes a bed for snow I have never been able to find out—usually these words are uttered on some still, mild afternoon. Ten to one, next morning when you are idly gazing out of the window, a single flake of white comes drifting and dancing out of the greyness. It clings, exquisite and precious, to the glass for a second or two—then it is a dull drop of water. It may be one flake in a small flurry, so that we say early in February, 'January was right mild this year'... Or it may be the precursor of millions, billions and trillions.

Sydney Goodsir Smith

23.1.1975

It is sad and strange that while this week we celebrate yet once more the birth of a great Scottish poet, we should pause and think of another one recently dead.

Sydney Goodsir Smith had more than a passing likeness to Robert Burns in many respects. He wrote, in Lallans too, poems in praise of love and whisky and Scotland. I am sure too he had many of Burns's personal characteristics—charm, humour, good-fellowship and the kind of charity that redeems everything. He was an altogether delightful man to be with. The 'howffs' along Rose Street in Edinburgh will be greatly the poorer for his death. There will never be his like again. He will pass now into the folklore of Scotland as one of its most gifted sons.

I make it an excuse for writing about Sydney Smith here (not that he needs an excuse—in any healthy society he would be a nationally acclaimed figure, cherished from Unst to Berwick-on-Tweed, and far beyond) the fact that he is known to more than a few Orkney folk, having visited the islands twice in the sixties with his charming wife Hazel. The first time, he stayed in Sanday and Stromness; the second time in Stromness. He loved the islands and spent much of his time drawing and sketching (for he was a talented artist too—for a time he was the art critic of *The Scotsman*). He told me how he breathed a rare 'euphoria' in Orkney. It was not in his nature to keep his happiness to himself—he had to splurge it around among his companions.

He seemed in many ways like one of those richly endowed characters out of eighteenth-century Scotland. One can imagine Burns's Edinburgh friends conversing in the same witty, learned, humorous, rounded periods as Sydney Smith, seasoned with mighty laughter and quotations from the classics.

He was more than a Scotsman, however. His birthplace was New Zealand, where his father had been Professor of Forensic Medicine before his appointment to Edinburgh University. Sydney got inspiration from all times and all cultures. Music and art helped to shape his work. He drew nourishment too from the new, exciting experiments in modern literature—Pound, Joyce, Jarry. He was a citizen of the world in the true sense.

His sequence of love poems, 'Under the Eildon Tree', and his prose epic 'Carotid Cornucopius', are precious additions to the sum of literature.

Burns, whom we celebrate this week, would be proud to receive Sydney Smith on the shores of *Tìr nan Òg*. I can imagine the heroic laughter of that meeting.

The Seller of Winds

30.1.1975

A winter storm in Orkney today. with occasional flurries of snow. blasts of wind round every corner, and even the sheltered harbour water flawed and darkened.

It was on a day like this, two hundred years ago, that the ale houses of Stromness would be full of stormbound sailors. And the ale house tills would rattle, and the leading townsfolk would be apprehensive, and Rev William Clouston would prepare a strong sermon for delivery the following Sabbath, with bits out of Virgil and Horace (for he was a great man for the classics).

The skippers would not be sitting at their grog in the common 'howffs'. They would be gathered in a superior inn, like Login's at the South End, exchanging news and snuffboxes; and discussing the serious situation in the American colonies of Virginia and Carolina; and describing the worsening storm in colourful sea-going language.

'I thought,' says one of them, 'that you had all been with your sixpences to that old trollop on the side of the hill.'...

The skippers look very embarrassed. They take mighty pinches of snuff into their nostrils, and a second or two later the inn is loud with faces exploding into spotted handkerchiefs. 'Maybe if you had gone too, captain,' says one of them with streaming eyes, 'the storm might have blown itself out in the night!'

They all laugh round the table with the jar of rum on it—half embarrassed, half hearty mirth...

But the scoffer declares that no old creature will get a brass farthing out of him! Control the weather indeed! Mistress Millie might go to blazes! The storm would end when the mighty cosmic forces that had caused it had shifted into another conjunction—not because an old wife boiled a kettle and muttered a few dark words in her hovel on the side of the hill.

* * *

The old woman[1], having counted once more the seven vessels lying at anchor in the Cairston Roads, and the half-dozen sixpences in her purse, took her shawl about her and felt her way down one of the steep closes into the town. From this ale house and that came noises of song and quarrelling. The old woman did not stop until she reached the inn where the skippers were yarning and drinking and taking snuff. Of course she didn't go in. She lingered in the rain at the door. Presently the skippers would come out, the six decent men and the one who had dared the mistress of the elements. Him she would fix with her ancient, sea-grey eye.

Freemen of Kirkwall

6.2.1975

Stromness, being a peedie place that has never acted host to royalty in the distant past, has not had the privilege of appointing 'Freemen'. But we ought to congratulate Kirkwall on its Freemen of the recent past. Mr Marwick[2] is a brilliant representative of Orkney culture, as Mr Scott[3] is of civic dignity.

---

1 Bessie Millie, prototype of Norna of Fitful Head, the ancient sybil in Scott's novel of Orkney and Shetland, *The Pirate*. She sold good winds to storm-bound skippers at sixpence a time. She was nearly a hundred years old when Scott talked to her in her hovel on the side of Brinkie's Brae.

2 Orkney scholar, historian, folklorist.

3 Ex-provost of Kirkwall.

It was intriguing, in last week's *Orcadian*, to read the list of honorary burgesses from the beginning. Most of them are now forgotten. Who was William Wauchope, who was enrolled in 1802? Or James Loch of Loudon in 1813? Or Henry Baxter in 1834? These are only three that have vanished into the great silence.

Stars of the finest magnitude shine out of the list. Sir Walter Scott was honoured in 1814. That was when he was touring the northern lighthouses on the *Pharos*. He never wasted an opportunity, Sir Walter. While he was in the north he gathered the material for his novel *The Pirate*. Having been made a Freeman of Kirkwall, it was a piece of rank ingratitude on his part to write those four scurrilous lines about the town. One would like to know the inside story—was somebody rude to him? Had he been slighted in some way?

The visit of Gladstone and Tennyson to Kirkwall has been well documented. By great good fortune the late John Mooney[1] was a young reporter at the time, and he 'covered' the Freedom ceremony. There was however only one speech, Gladstone's, to report. Tennyson, it seems, was in one of his austere, gloomy moods. It was 1883 when the greatest of the Victorian Prime Ministers and the greatest of her poets touched at Orkney—I think they were on a cruise to Russia.

It is pleasant to see that the City and Royal Burgh have, of recent decades, been very discriminating as to whom they honoured. No falling stars, who are here and gone again, like the aforementioned Wauchope and Loch and Baxter; but men of perennial merit, Sir James Marwick, Sir Thomas Clouston, Dr Campbell (Evie minister and Moderator of the General Assembly), John Mooney, Stanley Cursiter, Hugh Marwick—and lastly Ernest W. Marwick and James Scott. (Incidentally, it is interesting to note the number of Marwicks who shine in this galaxy; somebody, some day, will have to write an account of that highly talented family.)...

It is sad when a long tradition comes to an end. Is it not possible that Kirkwall Community Council could inherit some of the privileges of the almost defunct Town Council?

---

1 Historian, author of *St Magnus, Earl of Orkney*; *The Cathedral and Royal Burgh of Kirkwall*, etc.

A Great Triumvirate

13.2.1975

It was good to see yesterday in the Kirkwall Library the three bronze heads—Stanley Cursiter, Edwin Muir, Eric Linklater. I had seen Ian Scott's head of Stanley Cursiter before, of course, at the official unveiling in the Old Manse of Firth. The plaques do not give the names of the Muir and Linklater sculptors—at least I didn't notice any. It seems to be the head of the young Muir, but the wisdom and serenity of the mature poet are already there in the deep brow and dreaming mouth. It is the mature Linklater, surely; a head like Sweyn Asleifson[1] looking out from the prow of his ship—it is the last voyage—Ireland is there, just under the horizon.

It is a splendid idea to have that great triumvirate of artists in one place.

Yesterday was the first time I had been in Kirkwall for months. After a cold wet January it was a fine winter day—a cloudless sky and bronze light everywhere. You could almost feel the first tremors of spring; but if you stood still for five minutes the cold swords of winter still passed through you.

It was quite an afternoon. After viewing the bronzes in Kirkwall Library, we set out on the first circuit of the West Mainland of 1975. (There will be a score of circuits at least before autumn!)

After the car has spanned the flat plain of Rendall, it is always a joy to come on the sea, and Rousay, and beyond it, Eynhallow. Yesterday the 'roosts' were quiet and the sea was very blue. I pointed to a mountain in the ocean beyond Eynhallow and said 'Hether-Blether'[2]. But John Broom, who was driving the car, said it was a lump of sea-fog. He was probably right; all the Atlantic horizon was indistinct.

It wasn't a pure joyride we were on—it was serious business, the delivering of school textbooks to most of the peedie schools in the

---

1 Sweyn Asleifson, 'the ultimate Viking', died in Dublin, an old man, with a sword in his hand and a prayer in his mouth. Eric Linklater wrote memorably about that twelfth-century contemporary of Rognvald, earl and saint.

2 Eynhallow and Hether-Blether, 'the vanishing islands'. See the story of that name in *The Two Fiddlers* (Chatto and Windus).

West Mainland. In the playground of Birsay it was either the afternoon interval or lessons were over for the day. Children were playing hopscotch on the paving stones. Thank goodness, they still haven't got the brazen and defiant faces of many city children; they moved shyly away from the car when we drove in; and when we moved off again, after five minutes, we got enchanting smiles and hand-wavings.

When we drove down the Brae of Clouster into Stromness, the crest of Brinkie's Brae was a fountain of leaping gold. Then with one last serene upsurge the day-spring guttered and died. The sun was down.[1]

Slowly the fog that had been blurring the horizon all day moved in. When I went out that evening, the paving stones were wet; a cold sea haar had settled over the town. It was what the old folk called a 'raw' night. Winter was not yet over, because of this one good day.

The Door of Spring

6.3.1975

February is the shortest month and by reputation one of the nastiest. 'February fill-dyke'—what does that mean? I have an image of ditches drifted under with snow—and all the horrid business of the thaw to follow.

As I write, February has one day to go, and a fairer February I do not remember. Fancy the Pier Head seats being crowded with debaters and yarners on a February afternoon! But so they were today. The sun, mellowed with a faint mist, fell kindly over the Pier Head. It was a pleasure merely to sit and let that first faint warmth touch the blood. The harbour water was a shimmer of blue silk.

---

[1] I remember this day with gratitude and sadness, because it was the last time I spoke to my friend Charles Senior, poet and bookseller. He died two days later.

Then another new thing in the life of the town. Around two o'clock the *St Ola*—we are only slowly getting used to her huge bulk—entered the harbour, and turned herself around before backing into her berth. For the first time ever I watched cars and lorries being driven off and away.

Hard things have been said about February. But one of the pleasures of life, renewed each February, is the miracle of the lengthening day. Suddenly, late one afternoon, you realise that you are having tea by daylight. It seems only a step to the sweetness of May and June.

Today is the last day of winter (28th February) and so it is in my reckoning. Nobody has finally and forever fixed the border dates between season and season. Indeed, Henry MacKenzie, the forgotten but in-his-day celebrated Scottish novelist, says somewhere that it is a nonsense to speak of seasons at all in connection with a place like Orkney.

I'm sure that Orcadians are aware more than city dwellers of the four sovereign seasons. The men who built Brodgar and Maeshowe were acutely sensitive to the great dramas of light and darkness, seedtime and harvest.

We call December 21 midwinter because it is the darkest day; but I've always thought that in terms of coldness and storm that date stands much nearer the gateway of winter. For me, December-January-February is the kingdom of winter.

It is a delight to think that tomorrow, the first of March, spring begins.

February and winter are ending with kindness and serenity. There has been a full week now of sunshine—a thing we dare not expect even in July or August. Best not to girn about it and say, 'We'll pay for this yet!'... Just take the gold in hand and be thankful.

The Murmuring Shell

27.3.1975

You only realise that you are dull of hearing when you have to ask your friends to speak up, you didn't quite catch what they said then. And when the transistor battery doesn't last its usual two months, but you have to be buying another one in half that time. And when you have to switch up the TV to its highest (much, I'm sure, to the annoyance of the lieges). And when you meet folk on the street who say to you, mildly reproachful, 'I was at your door the other day and I knew you were in (for I heard the wireless going), but I got no answer to my knocking...'

You accept these things, along with blurring of vision, weariness of step, disinclination to go out of doors on a winter night, as a sign of the increasing years. Are we not all sentenced to end 'sans touch, sans smell, sans sight, sans everything'? The vivid outside world gradually ceases to impinge, with its swarming sounds and scents and colours. You have to withdraw into the hutch of yourself, and at last are a crotchety old man, a kind of third cousin to Scrooge.

It happened the other evening that I had to pay a visit to the doctor, about a matter which concerns nobody but himself and me. Suddenly, out of the blue, he asked, 'Are you deaf?' I said at once that I was, especially in the left ear.

'Something,' said he, 'can be done about that.'

We made an appointment for two evenings later. In the interim I was to take certain measures to soften up the pitch-clots in my ears.

The syringing of the ears is an awesome but on the whole pleasant operation. Great Niagaras of water thunder and shout through the auricles, a kind of Hallelujah Chorus, or a stampede of salmon up a river in full spate!... My friend the doctor washed out both ears, one after the other, while I held a kidney-bowl that kept filling and splashing over.

When it was all over I existed in a new world. Voices, that half an hour before were the dullest of whispers, sounded like the utterances of heroes. The tick of the clock, the fall of waves on the beach, even raindrops on the windowpane, came new and beautiful into the opened portals of the ear. In Edwin Muir's words, the whole world was 'rinsed and cleansed'. I seemed to stand in the centre of a delicate vibrating crystal bell.

There must be a hundred or two folk in Orkney, this very day, who have passed into the House of Middle Age where all is dimmer and duller than it was a decade ago. For their benefit I tell this true story. We may never be able to hear the thunders of the opening rose, or the delicate songs of dewfall, but at least we don't have to exist with stone ears in a world of stone.

*Also by George Mackay Brown from
Steve Savage Publishers*

Rockpools and Daffodils

(a Gordon Wright title)

Published in 1992, *Rockpools and Daffodils* is the third collection drawn from George Mackay Brown's weekly column in *The Orcadian*.

ISBN 0-903065-76-2

Hardcover. 28 colour photographs. RRP £14.95.

Available from bookshops or directly from the publisher.

For information on mail order terms, see our website (www.savagepublishers.com) or write to: Mail Order Dept., Steve Savage Publishers Ltd., The Old Truman Brewery, 91 Brick Lane, LONDON, E1 6QL.